D1588111

STARTLED
by
SILENCE

STARTLED
by
SILENCE

Finding God in Unexpected Places

Ruth Senter

CARMEL • NEW YORK 10512

This Guideposts edition is published by special arrangement
with Daybreak Books, Zondervan Publishing House.

STARTLED BY SILENCE
Copyright © 1986 by Ruth Senter

Edited and designed by Julie Ackerman Link

Printed in the United States of America

Against the Word the unstilled world still whirled
About the center of the silent Word.
    O my people, what have I done unto thee.
Where shall the word be found, where will the word
Resound? Not here, there is not enough silence.

—From *Ash-Wednesday*
by T. S. Eliot

Contents

Come with me
   Listen to the ordinary detail of your life
   Words not yet written
   Stories yet untold
   Empty spaces
   Blank pages
   Pictures not yet painted.

They are there
   If you will
   Pay attention
   To the silence
   Observe carefully
   Your space.
   For it
      Has spoken
      Is speaking
      Will speak
   If you will
      Listen
      Learn
      And write your own pages.

PART I: WHEN GOD SEEMS SILENT ... SILENCE SPEAKS

CHAPTER ONE

Unanswered Questions

What Do You Say?

*What do you say when the winds of
prejudice rip across your accomplishments
and scatter them like dried leaves in a
hurricane?*

*When someone else's insecurity plays
havoc with your personal comfort
because they:
misunderstand your actions,
misrepresent your position,
misread your statements?*

*No open-mindedness.
No questions asked.
just opinions of steel—
opinions set to destroy.*

*What do you say when you're the victim of
political power plays that toss you from
one judge to another?*

*Put you on trial when there's been
no offense,
pronounce you guilty without hearing
your side.
No justice.
No fairness.
just cold, crass politics—
to keep the power-wielders happy.*

*What do you say when the people you
trust most let you down in your
crisis hour?*

When they:

Sleep through the tensions
going on inside you,
sell you down the river for
their own personal profit,
slip out the side door and
leave you standing alone?

No sensitivity.
No empathy.
Just preoccupation with
their own safety and
comfort.

What do you say when you've been
Beaten by the system,
Stripped because of its
intolerance,
Nailed down because you don't
uphold the system's
interpretation of the truth?
Placed under lock and key because
it fears its own weaknesses?

What do you say?

Then they led Him to the place
called The Skull;
Executed Him among criminals.
And He said:
"Father, forgive them; for they know
not what they do."

(Luke 23:34)

God of the Jigsaw

"Don't try to figure me out, just love me," I said to Mark one day as he shook his head at me in absolute bewilderment. The cause of his perplexity has long since been forgotten, but the statement lives on.

I thought of it again when I read about how God dealt with the Israelites for worshiping the golden calf: "Go back and forth through the camp from one end to the other, each killing his brother and friend and neighbor" (Exodus 32:27). The Lord God of Israel said this to His people.

Harsh! Heartless! Cruel! I wanted to scream to my God of love, *"Where is Your mercy, Your forgiveness, Your grace?"*

I wanted to shout it again when I followed the coffin of a four-year-old neighbor; felt the slow, steady pulse of pain in my back; held the hand of a young widow left with two small children. Instead I simply shook my head in bewilderment, unable to understand an all-powerful God who, with a single gesture, can roll out the universe but who, when it comes to the lives of His children, sometimes appears not to lift a hand.

But I am not destroyed by God's mysterious ways. Here lies the foundation of my trust: I don't have to *understand* to *love*. To reduce God to a $5.98 jigsaw puzzle that I can put together, each piece in perfect place, would cheapen Him. It would reduce Him to my level.

In a world where we still must follow small coffins to cemeteries, we will never be able to understand or explain the enigma of a Man who lived thirty-three years in order to die; of a blinding light that revitalized body cells grown cold over three days, rolled a boulder from a cave, and conquered death once and for all.

I do not understand. But God is not diminished by my inability to reduce Him to a formula or to put Him together like a puzzle.

In fact, He wouldn't *be* God if He could be captured, contained, or perfectly understood (Isaiah 55:8). He would be mortal—and I could not give my life, my loyalty, my unreserved allegiance to anyone as finite as myself.

It is His mystery that inspires me to worship, to explore His depths, and to confess that I can't always fit together the pieces of His ways. There are times, through the silence, when I can almost hear Him say, "Ruth, don't try to figure Me out. Just love Me."

Looking Away

 He stood alone in a sheltered spot where two walls
came together, his hands in his pockets, his slanted eyes
staring blankly into nothing. I looked twice. Who was he
and what was he doing here at this time of the morning?

"You need some help?"

I could see the whites of his eyes as he looked my
direction. He nodded and with the back of his hand wiped
the saliva that was seeping form his mouth. I wanted to
turn away but I knew I was already committed.

"Let's see if we can't find your class." I took his short,
stubby hand and guided him down the hall.

He's all wrong, I thought to myself as we walked
together. So obviously wrong. A head that is way too small for
his body. A nose that is too flat. Ears and teeth that are not the
right size. Eyes slanted in the wrong direction.

Rounding the corner into Wing B, we met my friend

Sue. Her eyes did a quick scan of my companion, then she looked the other way. She never even saw I was there. I opened my mouth to speak but she was gone.

Sue had never passed by me before. We always had a million things to say to each other and never enough time to say them all. But today it was as though I were invisible.

As my companion and I continued toward the classroom for handicapped children, no one in those usually friendly halls showed any signs of recognizing me. I was baffled. These were the halls of my church. People always talked to me.

Then it struck me. People weren't seeing me because of the mongoloid child at my side. Did distorted bodies make them so uncomfortable that they had to turn the other direction?

"Lonely world, isn't it, little fellow?" I thought to myself as I patted him on the head and delivered him safely to his teacher.

My walk down the hall with a mongoloid child didn't end that day—at least not in my mind. I realized that except for my curiosity and noble feelings that prompted me to be a Good Samaritan, I too would have looked the other way.

I've done it much of my life: the time a man in front of me at church had an epileptic convulsion; when my brother fell on a rock and ripped his head wide open; and when I walked among the grotesque forms of humanity that slumped over brown bottles in the streets of New York's Bowery.

I would rather life didn't paint such unattractive pictures. I prefer happiness and normalcy. I would rather not see a man without legs or a woman with a hole in her throat and a tube sticking out so she can talk. I prefer not to have to stand by a casket and face the cold, lifeless body of my four-year-old neighbor who used to run through our front yard and swing on our porch swing.

Although God does not hold me responsible for figuring out the reasons for life's distortions, I am responsible for how I respond to them, because Jesus taught me the correct response. He did not turn off the ugly side of life or look the other way. He didn't go into hibernation, indifferent to suffering people. Instead, he reached out and touched people's abnormalities. He gave sanity to a boy with an evil spirit who lay on the ground foaming at the mouth and slashing himself with stones. He placed his hands on a leper—His society's most abhorred outcasts—and pronounced him clean. He took Jairus's dead daughter by the hand and said, "My child, get up." Jesus touched the most ugly sores of humanity and used His power to change them.

I didn't change anything about the little mongoloid boy that Sunday morning when I helped him find his room. He will probably drool and roll his eyes all his life. His head will never get any larger nor his nose any longer. But perhaps my silent act of taking his wet, stubby hand in mine somehow said to him, "You are a valuable and special part of God's world. I can no longer afford to look the other way."

Beyond the Superficial

"Why don't they get that kid's eyes fixed. Don't his parents realize he hasn't got a chance looking like that?"

I winced at the stranger's thoughtless words. That was my *friend* she was talking about. Lovable, huggable, four-year-old Jonathan. Every time he saw me, he called out, "Root! Root! Can I come to your house today?" Then he'd shuffle toward me, his little body leaning too far to one side, and reach out for me. His brown eyes were always smiling. I'd stoop down and hug him, hoping somehow he could feel my squeeze through the hard plastic brace that had housed his body since he was fourteen months old.

I looked at his mother and hoped she hadn't heard. She was patiently coaching Jonathan's little hands as they struggled for control while ice cream trickled down his chin. She had been his patient coach since the doctors shook their heads years before. They extended their sympathy after using such frightening terms as cerebral palsy, severe mental retardation, hypotonic, no muscle control, institutionalization.

The fight to overcome had been long and hard. Jonathan's mother had met all the obstacles with courage. The fact that her son walked and talked at all was a monument to her patience and perseverance.

But no one asked about Jonathan's mother's courage today. No one spoke of the hope that had sustained her through the dark months of hurt and disappointment. No one seemed to care how it felt to wipe melting ice cream off your son's chin while other boys his age quickly gobbled up every bit of the cool refreshment, refusing to leave even a drop on their chins or in the cone, and then tore off to ride their bicycles down narrow sidewalks or to skip lightly over cracks in the sidewalk.

No one seemed to wonder, either, what life was like for my little friend. They never got beyond his eyes.

I thought that day of the One who is far less concerned with what is outside than He is with what is *inside*. Jesus Christ looks beyond the superficial. He is much more aware of how people feel than how they look.

One day He saw emptiness. He didn't mind that it resided in the heart of a Samaritan woman, who Jewish religious leaders refused to even look upon. Jesus, uninhibited by their prejudices, stopped, talked, and ministered to her need. The woman was surprised; so were His disciples (John 4:9, 27). But externals didn't matter to God's Son. No wonder people were healed by His touch.

I walked over and held Jonathan's little hand, still sticky from the ice cream. His large brown eyes smiled up at me. Funny, I'd forgotten that his eyes were crossed.

The Misfit

His life goes out with a bang.
The crowds gather
Spectators cheer
And death hawks its wares.
Cheap flesh
A common criminal
Small town boy
With grand illusions
And lofty dreams about his own identity.
Society has a place for people who lose
    touch with reality.
White coats
Black robes
Iron bars
Unstained wood that drips blood.
And so "The Misfit" meets his final foe
Surrenders up his soul
And dies.
Conquered
Contained

UNANSWERED QUESTIONS

Put in his place.
In the west the sun sets
And darkness disperses the crowd.
But in this place of dead-men's bones
The earth groans with the weight that it
  bears
A form unfit for death
Designed for life.
The rocks cry out
They roll away.
Concrete slabs split in two
While the earth rejects what it cannot
  rightfully keep.
Nature reverses its flow
rids itself of its terrible crime.

"The Misfit" shakes eternity.
For every eye shall see
Every knee shall bow.
And in the east, The Son rises
And His rays light the whole world.

Why Pray?

Surely God already knows what He's going to do with my life, so why should I pray? Within the split second it took the heavy-duty utility truck to plow past the yield sign and into my path—brakes screeching, metal interlocking, and glass flying—I knew I'd found my answer.

Just twenty-four hours earlier I had said good-bye to a group of new friends in Seattle and had boarded a plane for home. We had been together for three days in the peaceful fir country west of Puget Sound.

Most of us met as strangers at that retreat. We had prayed together in small groups, not because we felt any great need but because the schedule called for it. In the beginning no one said much. Polite formalities only, nothing private or personal.

But over steaming cups of tea and homemade cinnamon rolls, we laid aside our façades. We walked together down quiet paths among the giant firs and left behind our concerns about what others might think.

Against the green of the forest or along streams of blue, hurts emerged. Pain—some old, some new—was expressed. Disappointments of yesterday. Hopes for tomorrow. Gradually we began to catch sight of the people behind the faces.

In the end, we didn't have enough hours to say it all. As we joined hands and formed a prayer pact, we promised to pray especially for each other during the following twenty-four hours.

My friends gathered around me for a final farewell. "Lord," one prayed, "during this next day, put Your wall of protection around Ruth. We know the lows often come just after the highs. Keep Ruth—mentally, physically, and spiritually—during these next twenty-four hours."

We hugged each other, waved a final good-bye, and I began the long flight home.

My plane lifted off at 1:05 on Wednesday afternoon. Thursday afternoon, just before the twenty-four-hour period ended, the utility truck plowed through the yield sign, nearly totaling my car. I walked away with bruises and an aching back.

Why pray? Because the schedule calls for it—prayer is an act of obedience. Sometimes, even when friends pray, utility truck drivers fail to yield the right of way. I am not responsible for the results of prayer. I am only responsible to obey. Why pray? I'm not sure, except God tells me to. And for me, that's reason enough.

Listen to the unanswered questions in your life.
What do you hear?

CHAPTER TWO

Life and Death

God Is So Good?

Yesterday was tangle-free.
My day was peaceful and predictable.
Consistent with a God of love,
> *The birds sang,*
> *The sun shone,*
> *The children obeyed.*
> *My neighbor across the street extended her Christianity to me*
> > *with a loaf of bread still warm from her oven.*
> *And I*
> *Hugged my children,*
> *Opened my arms wide to the sun,*
> *Bit deeply into the freshness of rye and melted butter.*
> *Aloud I said, "God is so good."*

That was yesterday.
> *Today I stumble in a tangled web of confusion and disorder.*
> *Jori met me at the front door with the staggering message:*
> > *"Mom, Katherine died."*
> *My friend Katherine—*
> > *one of my partners in Tuesday morning Bible study—*
> > *dead!*
> *My brain staggered with the weighty information.*
> > *I had no place to put it.*
> > *No mental file designated*
> > > *"Death of a friend;*
> > > *mother of a twenty-four-hour-old infant."*
> *Suddenly I am a stranger in my own house,*
> > *lost in my own kitchen.*
> *It doesn't fit. It just doesn't fit!*
> > *The birth was so ordinary. So easy.*

Why the sudden headache? Why the coma?
Why the death at all?
Why? Why? Why?
I move through the reality of Katherine's death—
    a tangled jumble of emotions, physical symptoms, questions.

God is good?

I look at the newborn, asleep in his motherless room.
I reach out and take the hand of the grieving father.
    "I'm so sorry. Katherine was a special person."
I tell him about the rainy morning she called me.
    "You have a lot to do for the brunch," she had said.
    "Let me come early and help you get ready."
For a moment her husband and I are bound together
    in the happy memory of when Katherine was with us.
I leave my basket of fruit and cheese on the kitchen table
    and slip out the side door.
Katherine's two older boys are coming home from the neighbor's.
    The three-year-old clutches a stuffed puppy in his arms.
    His five-year-old brother walks by me with his eyes lowered.

God is good?

Three motherless boys.
    An empty rocking chair.
    A daddy alone.
I drive home wondering. I feel knots inside and out.
At last I say aloud, "Yes, God is still good.
    I have no alternative but to believe Him.
    Even when I can't understand."

Warm Days and Tombstones

The day had a life and death irony about it. Warm June sun and stone-cold concrete. Bursts of new life—petunias, geraniums, and lilies-of-the-valley—marking the passing of the seasons. Final epitaphs—names, dates, and family links—marking the passing of the generations.

"Mellinger's Mennonite Church." We slowed the car as we approached the sign and turned right into the parking lot. For my mother, this place was not only a house of God but also a house of childhood memories. In a sense, she was home. Cradled on the grassy slopes that surrounded the old, red brick structure were her people: the Diffenbaughs, the Martins, the Goods, the Mellingers. We moved among the memories of flesh and blood; among names I knew from the Old German Family Bible on Mother's coffee table at home. I reached down and touched the marble, rubbed my hand over block letters smoothed by time. She only lived to be twenty-eight. She was the grandmother I had never known. Dead of tuberculosis when my mother was only four.

There was no granite and marble on the upper slopes—only summer's spread of grass, deep green arborvitae, and a sprawling oak tree or two. I felt I was walking from past into future. I knew someday I'd stand on these same slopes and touch death closeup. Someday it would no longer be the vague ancestors of another generation buried here, but those with whom I'd shared life.

"Plots 43 through 46. Right here under this oak." The cemetery caretaker stopped at the far end of the ridge. We looked down on the peaceful valley of marble and concrete.

"What a beautiful view," my mother said. She was facing the church and the gentle hills beyond. "Just right for the resurrection," my dad added. His voice was confident and calm. I watched his steady hand as he signed the contract. "Hollinger. Plots 43, 44, 45, 46." He screwed the top back on his pen, folded the paper, and put it into his portfolio for safekeeping. We had agreed on our immortality. Now we could go home.

"Only the person who is not afraid to die is the person who is not afraid to live." I thought of General MacArthur's words as we turned out of Mellinger's Cemetery and headed home. Someday Mellinger's Cemetery will be a place, not of final defeat, but of ultimate victory. Today we had taken one step toward that day of triumph.

Randy's Song

Sometimes it's hard to sing.

I could tell Nicky was struggling with tears. He was singing Randy's song. In fact, all of the evening's music belonged to Randy; it was a memorial to an eight-year old classmate who had slipped beneath the dark waters of an ice-jammed lake and never again opened his eyes. Father, son, and snowmobile had been pulled from the frigid water the following day.

"Randy's dead," was all Nick said that fateful day when he walked in from school. As I gathered him into my arms, his grief came pouring out—grief that streaked his cheeks and splashed my blouse where I held him. Then words came. Slowly. Thoughtfully. Through the afternoon and on into the night.

"Randy and I were going to the pros together." We looked at the football team picture that hung on his bedroom wall. "Carol Stream Panthers, 70-Pounders, 1982." Nick and Randy stood together.

"I feel like God didn't answer my prayer. I prayed so hard that he wouldn't die . . . He was my best friend, next to Trey . . ." He straightened himself up and reached for another tissue. "I have to go and say good-bye to him on Sunday."

Now, two days after his final farewell to Randy, Nick stood and sang for his friend.

"I wish Randy was here tonight," he had said as he dressed for the evening. "Mom, why do you think God let him die?"

It was another of his questions for which I had no easy, made-to-order response. So I simply said, "Nicky, sometimes life is like looking into a mirror in a dark room. We can't see our reflection because of the dark. Someday when we see God we'll understand Randy's death."

I pointed to 1 Corinthians 13:12. "Until then," I said, "we'll just have to be content not to understand." He nodded his assent.

"I didn't really feel like singing tonight," Nick said later that evening as I tucked him into bed. "But I did it anyhow."

"And Nicky," I answered through the dark, "sometimes we *have* to sing even when we don't feel like it."

He sighed deeply. "Yep. I guess so." He turned over and hugged his pillow like he always does when he's ready for sleep.

I knew Randy's song was preparing him for life's next disappointment.

On Learning of a Friend's Terminal Cancer

The shadow
Like icy claws of dark
Oozes through the cracks
Of my spirit
Where no sunshine is.
It presses hard
Against
   Reason
   Logic
   Sense.
It makes no sense.
There is no sense
In shadows.
Only
   Fear
   Unknown
   None light.
Scary figures on the wall
Which is the darkest of them all?

ON LEARNING OF A FRIEND'S TERMINAL CANCER

"Yea though I walk . . . "
I walk through the shadow.
Hide and seek
But mostly hide.
Black and gray
But mostly black.
Life and death
But mostly death.
Through the shadow
I walk.
There is no light.
Only a Hand.

Family Reunion

August was unusually warm. It hung in hot, heavy masses and clung to our skin like a steamy comforter. Even central Pennsylvania felt like the tropics.

No one wanted to move. We sat in the shade of the front porch, drank ice lemonade, and waited for the oscillating fan to turn our way. Every ounce of energy was spent fighting the heat.

When Mother finally suggested it was time for us all to get ready for the reunion, I groaned inwardly. A conclave of the generations on a one-hundred-degree day sounded anything but appealing. Uncles. Great aunts. Grandpa's Daddy's sister. Aunt Fannie's oldest child with Grandpa's eyes. First, second, and third cousins. Faces and forms I hadn't seen for fifteen years and probably wouldn't see for another ten. What did it matter? We lived different places, went separate ways, and, except for the hereditary thread that tied us together, had very little in common.

What's so important about eating sandwiches with second cousins once removed and wiping sweat, swatting flies, and slapping mosquitoes. But here I was, sitting on a hard, backless picnic bench, swatting flies and swapping stories about the good old days.

Uncle Phares told most of the stories. For a time, I forgot the heat, flies, and mosquitoes and remembered only that he and my dad were once boys together. He pulled out his box of old black-and-white snapshots of little boys riding horses, jumping through hoops, and dressed in knickers, white shirts, and suspenders.

Next was Europe, Uncle Phares' more recent pictorial update. I eagerly leaned over the table and looked at pictures until my back ached and I thought I'd never walk straight again. But I felt as if I knew Uncle Phares. My own flesh and blood. Funny how I'd never noticed before that he looked so much like my dad.

In October mother's phone call told of Uncle Phares' death. Suddenly I was back in that one-hundred-degree meadow, in a sense, paying my final respects to Uncle Phares. It would have been easier not to go. But when you're a family you go out of your way for each other—the way God did for His family. Today, I'm very glad that on that hot August day, I did.

What Do You Say
to a Dying Man?

The call I'd been expecting
came today. "Art died," the
church secretary said. I wasn't surprised, but now that the
time had come I couldn't think of anything to say.

I thought back to an evening not long ago when Mark
and I dropped by to see Art. The snow crunched under our
boots and the Christmas lights winked from the front
windows as we walked to the door. The house looked
happy enough from the outside, but inside was the sober
realization that this would probably be Art's last Christmas.

"Come on in." He greeted us cheerfully from his
hospital bed in the corner of the living room. His thin
hand motioned to the piano bench that was beside his bed.
I couldn't help but think how often I had seen those same
hands, strong and sure, bring piano keys to life. Now his

baby grand sat in the corner like a slumbering giant, and his muted trumpet rested on its stand at the foot of his bed.

What do you say to a dying man? I had come with all kinds of encouraging words and ideas of things to talk about. I meant to ask about the music camp he directed last summer, the book he wrote last year, and his daughter's wedding coming up in April. I never got to my list.

"It's not easy giving up your instruments . . . kind of like saying good-bye to life-long friends . . . Rosemary's in the kitchen . . . Say hello to her . . . She's a fine woman . . . worked herself to exhaustion planning a surprise party for my fiftieth birthday last week . . . Birthdays can be traumatic . . . So is cancer . . . Hardest thing is the pain and the medication . . . makes you a stranger to yourself . . . Sometimes you have no idea why you say or do things . . . almost like you're another person . . ."

Art talked on. His words began to slow down. I could tell he was getting tired. We stood to go.

"Thanks for coming," he said. "You've been a real encouragement to me."

Mark and I squeezed his hand and said good-bye.

We encouraged him? I thought to myself as we walked to the car. *We didn't even say anything.*

Then I realized we'd *listened* rather than talked— probably the best thing we possibly could have done for a dying man.

Reason to Celebrate

Cameras scan the wide, white door decked with garlands of green, then zoom in on a fire blazing on the hearth. Silver bells and mistletoe. Joyful songs float from a baby grand piano. Happy faces gaze at the treasures piled beneath a huge spruce tree. The setting is idyllic. Mothers and fathers, grandpas and grandmas, glide through the room. Holding hands, hugging, laughing, sipping wassail from silver cups. All is bliss and happiness.

I sit in my living room watching the TV fantasy. Across the street my neighbor's lights burn into the night. Police cars come and go. Their only daughter, twenty-year-old Julie, who disappeared while en route to work, has been found five miles away. Dead of gunshot wounds . . .

"Joy to the world, the Lord is come." The sound of singing fills the halls of the nursing home. I walk through a semi-dark room and take the hand gripping a bedrail.

"Merry Christmas." Her eyes blink open for a minute or two.

"Do I know you?" Her tired face shuts down again.

"No. You don't know me. I'm just here to say 'God bless you.'" This time she groans and turns her head toward the wall where a photograph smiles down at her. The man's face looks distinguished and gentle. I wonder where he is tonight . . .

I push a buzzer and wait. Second floor, east wing is quiet on Christmas Eve. Too quiet. Through an intercom on the wall, a squeaky voice asks for my credentials. Then the thick door to the psychiatric ward swings open. I walk through in search of my friend. She is singing with the other residents of second east, "'Tis the season to be jolly."

Soon the carols end and carolers shuffle down the hall like robots. They turn into their rooms and close their doors on each other.

My friend and I sit on the edge of her bed and talk. Her speech is slow. Her mind seems to be racing to catch up. I pray with her, then leave my tray of cookies on her nightstand next to the picture of her seven-year-old. She hugs me and I see that her eyes are misty. We walk together to the end of the hall. The heavy steel door closes behind me. Tomorrow is December 25.

As I light the last candle on our advent wreath I think of Bethlehem's Child, born in the shadow of a cross. No fantasy world of silver bells and mistletoe, just the cold realities of life and death. But I celebrate anyhow. I light my candles and sing my carols because Christ has come to wrap the grim realities of life with purpose. Significance. Meaning. Reason enough to celebrate.

Listen to the life and death that touches you.
What do you hear?

CHAPTER THREE

Pain

Suffering Reconsidered

You came to me
Not in downy, soft blankets,
   White, sterile sheets,
   Or antiseptic incubator.
They didn't close Your windows
   To keep out the germs;
Spray "white lace and roses"
   To improve Your air;
Inoculate You at 18 months
   To kill potential viruses.

But You touched the earth
   Where the air hung heavy with animal waste
   And the wind blew cold between the cracks;
   Hard splinters,
   Rough, coarse hay Your bed.
You lived among splinters of wood and
   iron spikes.
But You reached for life
   Without protection.
   Drank of the dust.
   Breathed its pollution.
You moved among earth's viruses
   And touched its sores.
And when Your last great enemy, death,
Tore You from the One who loved You most,

You agonized alone.
"My God, My God, why have You forsaken Me?"
Ultimate pain—the pain of rejection.

Tonight I kneel in the garden of my own Gethsemane.
"Father, if it be possible, remove this cup from me."
But the heavens are mute.
R.S.V.P. request in a dead-letter file.
There is no answer.
Pain stalks the broken vertebra of my back
    and sticks a thousand needles into my toes.
There is no relief.
I cower in the shadows of a sleepless night
In my downy, soft blankets,
    White, sterile sheets,
    And thermostatically-controlled air.
I reach for the doctor's prescription
    To dull the pain
As I pray for deliverance.
While on a hill outside of town
Your skies remained silent;
The Father turned His back.
Pain conquered.
For a while.
Who am I to claim exemption?

Delicate Surgery

I stared straight up at the pattern in the ceiling tiles as the high-intensity lamp glared down at me. The hand at the other end of my arm seemed to belong to someone other than myself. But the clanking of instruments on sterile trays and the strong smell of alcohol reminded me that the hand the doctor was about to repair was indeed mine. I took a deep breath and braced myself for the ordeal.

"A little nervous?" Dr. Wood's voice was calm, yet concerned. "A few more minutes and you won't feel the pain." He gently probed the wreckage at the tips of my fingers. "Mean storm window, I'd say," he exclaimed. "Must have fallen hard!"

I felt he understood my hurt.

"It could have been much worse," I offered, trying to talk myself into bravery. My mind retrieved a news story

I'd read months earlier about this hospital and an eighteen-year-old whose severed hand had been reattached. It was a story of amazing skill. After ten hours of surgery and the use of a microscope that magnified small vessels to forty times their original size, the doctors had restored veins, arteries, tendons, tissues, and nerves with sutures measuring half the diameter of a human hair! Suddenly I had complete trust in the man who bent over my left hand and gently repaired the damaged ends of my fingers.

Several weeks have passed since that hospital visit, and my fingers are healing. But today as I read through Paul's letter to the church at Galatia, I was reminded again of my doctor's skill.

The word *restore* stands out on the page. "Brothers," Paul writes, "if someone is caught in a sin, you who are spiritual should *restore* him gently" (Gal. 6:1).

"Restore," I learn, is a translation of the Greek word *katartizo*, which in Paul's day was a medical term meaning "to mend" or "to set bones," an action requiring great skill.

I've read Galatians 6:1 many times before. But today for the first time I understand the gentleness, the thoughtful care, and the sensitivity to hurt that is required of me if I am to help restore a brother or sister who has stumbled over some spiritual obstacle. Spiritual pain can be just as deep as physical hurt. Both require gentle care and sensitivity for healing to occur. Dr. Wood's gentle care reminded me of my responsibility.

Peace and Pain

The day started peacefully enough. English muffins and orange juice on the patio. No movement except a flutter of leaves now and then and a cardinal munching its breakfast at the bird feeder. In my Bible I read about peace—peace for my children. I underlined the verse and marked it: Promise for today: "All your sons will be taught by the Lord, and great will be your children's peace . . . and you will have nothing to fear" (Isa. 54:13–14).

"Come quick! Nicky's hurt." The words of my son's friend Scotty tumbled out in a frightened little wail. "There's blood gushing from his foot."

I'd watched Nicky and friends disappear down the street ten minutes before. They were running in the grass alongside a fire truck that was checking fire hydrants.

"Lord, keep us all calm," I prayed as I raced toward the scene. An assortment of firemen and children huddled around Nicky. A police car pulled in behind the big red fire truck. Down the hill came the paramedic truck, lights flashing, siren wailing.

"Deep laceration," the paramedic said as he cleaned the wound and applied pressure to stop the bleeding. "E.R. should handle it just fine. You want us to run him in or do you want to take him?"

Nicky's face looked white against the green grass. "I'll take him," I said, trying to sound calm.

When it was just the two of us on our way to the hospital Nicky spoke. He'd been brave; now he could cry. "Mommy," his voice quivered. "Mommy. My all-star game. It's day after tomorrow. Will I be OK by then?"

We both knew he wouldn't. I saw the pain in his blue eyes—not a deep kind of pain, but the kind that comes when your heart has held a dream for a long time and suddenly it is snatched away. His tears came unchecked.

"Nicky, I'm sorry." I took his little hand in mine. "You know Nicky, sometimes God teaches us the most through our disappointments. But it still hurts, doesn't it?"

Later that week, with his bandaged foot propped up in front of him, Nicky watched the Little League all-star game from the sidelines. He was trying hard to be brave, but I knew the pain he felt. It hurt to see him suffer.

Then I recalled the promise I'd read in Isaiah: "Your sons shall be taught by the Lord, and great will be your children's peace." I reviewed what I already understood—that God sometimes takes my children through pain in order to teach them about peace. It was up to me to simply trust God's style of instruction for Nicky.

Nicky's foot healed quickly. Only a small scar lingers as a silent reminder of God's lesson.

About Your Timing, Lord . . .

My doctor's words over the phone left me stunned. "Ruth, the mammogram has revealed a suspicious mass in your left breast. I want you to see a surgeon."

Standing there in the middle of my kitchen that cold November day I suddenly felt alone, forsaken. *God, did You forget? I'm the one who is just getting over a car accident. Remember? I was hit by that utility truck three weeks ago tomorrow. About Your timing, Lord . . .*

I struggled to replay the doctor's phone conversation to Mark, but the words got hung up on my emotions.

"I'm not sure I could ever face anything like that," I'd always said when anyone had talked about breast cancer experiences to me. Two of my aunts had died of that dread disease, so such stories always hit much too close to home. Now that the storyline *had* come home, my mind was desperately trying to decide what to do with it.

Suddenly, it was as though I were watching a performance on a screen, except *I* was in the picture. I saw myself responding to Mark's strong arms of comfort, steadying my voice, wiping my eyes, taking a deep breath.

"God will give us courage to face whatever we have to face," I said. "Right now it's time to take the children to school. Please don't worry. I'll be all right. I'll call the surgeon this morning."

I could tell he didn't want to leave, but his classes were waiting. I waved him out the door.

Two weeks later I lay in my hospital bed watching the flurry of activity around me. Another hour and the surgeon would begin his exploration, removing the mass and carefully searching for life-or-death cells.

"Just a little something to help you relax." The nurse took the syringe from the tray she carried. The needle did its work.

Fifteen minutes later she returned. "Ruth, are you asleep already? That shot worked fast on you. Probably because you've been so relaxed all along." She gently lifted my arm and took my pulse. I knew she was talking about resources I didn't have on my own.

Later, after the test results came back marked benign, I thought back to that cold November day when the doctor first called and to the morning of surgery when the countdown was at one hour. I recalled how miraculously and silently God's peace changed from something I talked about to something I knew for a fact. Sometimes there is no other way to learn.

Listen to the pain of your life.
What do you hear?

PART II: WHEN I AM SILENT ... GOD SPEAKS

CHAPTER FOUR

Interruptions

Please Interrupt

Sometimes I feel like an interruption,
and then I want to shrink
back into my shell
and never come out again.
I want to walk away and say,
"I'm sorry I took your time."

Being an interruption hurts.
It tells me
something is more important than I am.
It tells me
to hurry up and move along.
It tells me
you are looking
but don't see me.
It tells me
you are listening

but don't hear me.
And so I move along.

But, God says,
"Don't hurry away.
Stick around.
Tell me how it is with you.
Tell me what you're feeling
  right this minute.
Tell me why you feel that way.
I want to know you.
You count with me.
I care about you.
Tell me what I can do for you."

And I go away feeling
  He was glad I called.

Stranger in My House

I sat up in bed. I wasn't dreaming; there *were* voices coming from my kitchen. What was going on at 12:30 in the morning? I didn't have to wonder long. Mark came into the bedroom to reassure me.

"It's Tom," he explained in a whisper. "He's been drinking again. This time the police nabbed him for driving while under the influence. He has nowhere else to go. Some good hot coffee will sober him up. Then I'll put him to bed on the family room couch."

I stared at my pastor-husband through the 12:30 A.M. haze. "He's drunk, and you brought him *here?*" I didn't even know the man—except that he was somebody's uncle and Mark was trying to help him. My mind immediately shifted into high gear.

You can never tell with strangers—especially when they've been drinking. I've heard stories on the news about people who trusted strangers and were murdered or brutally assaulted. You can't trust people you don't know. What about the kids? What if they get hurt? And what about our valuables?

After Mark returned to the kitchen, I watched the glowing green hands of my alarm clock crawl through the early morning hours and waited for the inevitable outburst of violence. None came. I smelled coffee and heard Mark's calm voice.

Finally the house was quiet. Mark came to bed, but for me sleep did not come. I felt the presence of the stranger in my house. I had entertained guests many times. I prided myself on always having my coffeepot plugged in and my favorite brand of muffins stockpiled in the freezer for unexpected drop-ins.

Tonight we had had an unexpected drop-in. Why was he so hard to accept? Were my blueberry muffins and Columbian coffee only to be served to my kind of people? Did my front porch doormat say "Welcome" only to those I knew and loved? Could only "safe" people sit and rest in my walnut rocker?

From somewhere in the back of my mind came Christ's penetrating questions of Matthew 5:46–47 NASB: "For if you love those who love you, what reward have you? . . . And if you greet your brothers only, what do you do more than others?"

I concluded that my Christianity isn't very credible if my coffeepot is always hot for friends who drop by, but my house is cold to strangers. Christianity is unique because it causes us to bring out our best coffee and blueberry muffins and offer them to strangers in need. Christianity is unique because it silently yet powerfully urges us to forget ourselves and think of others—even when it happens to be someone's uncle who has had too much to drink.

The Wasteland

"It's hard to withstand an enemy when you don't know
. . . who he is or how he operates. Unexpected enemies are
our greatest foes." The United States General looked tired
and worn. Three agonizing weeks ago a member of the
overseas diplomatic corps had disappeared. While walking
from his home toward the American Embassy, with
American soldiers practicing drills at a nearby base, he was
snatched into oblivion.

The General spoke of political and military maneu-
vers, but he could just as well have been speaking of
spiritual operations, the similarities were so obvious.
Ignorance of the opposition always leaves room for surprise
attacks. And surprise attacks often end in defeat.

One distinguishing fact about spiritual conflict is that
it is usually most intense just after victory. It happened
that way with Jesus. He had just received the Holy Spirit,

God's stamp of approval, signifying that He was qualified
for His assignment. Then came the wilderness—the harsh,
barren wasteland west of the Jordan Valley. For the Son of
God, the wasteland followed the victory celebration.

I have seen similar patterns in my own life and
remember one instance in particular. For three days I had
given my all during a retreat for pastors' wives. The women
had been warm and generous. They applauded my stories
about how I was learning to share my husband when others
needed him, and complimented my three-point outlines
on gracious giving and flexibility.

"It's where you've lived," they said when it was all
over. "We can tell." I flew home in the clouds, aware of
God's enablement.

I was still in the clouds the next day when our family
set out for homecoming festivities at a nearby college. The
happiest thing about the day was that we were all together.

Together, that is, until one of our parishioners spotted
my husband as we headed for the football field. "Oh,
Mark, Grace needs you right away! Please go to her. She's
terribly frightened."

Immediately I felt the wasteland. The sun was
scorching and the mountaintops were far away. I walked
alone with the children toward the game. *Hadn't I shared
Mark enough? Couldn't we have just one day together this
week?* My giving was no longer gracious. My "flexibility"
had turned to steel, my day to gray.

As we squeezed into a bleacher full of bodies, I
suddenly realized that this was where my tidy three-point
outlines would either stand or fall. God's test for me was
not to be on the mountaintop but in the wilderness.

Then it hit me: The enemy is smart enough to know
that my lofty times are also my most vulnerable. Next time
I won't be so surprised at his silent, subtle strategy.

Sermon in an Airport

O'Hare airport can be a fun place when everything is on schedule. But on a Friday night in the middle of a blinding, Midwest blizzard, when flights are being delayed, re-routed, and canceled, it can be like a bad dream come true, especially with two impatient children who are anxious for Daddy to come home.

I had exhausted my supply of things to do with my nine- and five-year-old: We had played hide-and-seek through rows of semi-enclosed telephone booths, follow-the-leader up and down the escalators, and hopscotch on the square tiles at the end of Concourse C.

Time crawled through the two-and-a-half hours. Nothing changed on the arrival monitors. The crowds were restless. So were we. Thoughts turned toward home—a hot dinner and a warm bed.

I left home expecting a quick pickup at the airport and

nothing more, but the blizzard had caught up with us. There was a storm between the airport and home, a flight from Denver somewhere overhead, two hungry, tired children by my side, and $2.04 in my purse. We had just enough money to get us out of the parking garage, yet I knew we needed food.

"I'll have two scoops of chocolate ice cream, please, and three glasses of water," I half whispered to the waitress in the coffee shop. I'd figured carefully. With tax, the bill would come to $1.78.

"But, Mommy, we'll have to spend the night in the parking garage." Nine-year-old Jori's face showed signs of panic. "We don't have enough money to get out!"

"Let's wait and see," I whispered, trying to use my most confident, cheerful voice. "Eat your ice cream," I said as visions of an all-night airport camp-out filled my mind.

Finally I motioned to the waitress for our bill.

"You're taken care of," she said, smiling as though she were in on a secret. "The couple over there picked up your tab when they left."

I felt as if someone had just given me a warm hug on a cold night. *Who were those people disappearing from my view? And why did they do this for us?* All I had noticed about them was that one had been wearing a white fur coat. That was all I would ever know about either of them.

I looked at the children across the table. "God says we shouldn't worry about what we're going to eat because He knows even before we do what we will need. I guess when He said it, He really meant it, didn't He?"

Jori and Nicky nodded, their eyes wide with excitement. I knew we would never forget that snowy night and God's silent sermon assuring us of His care and provision.

The Chocolate Monster

The Saturday evening routine was typical for our family—no hint of the extraordinary. I hurried the children through their usual bathing and hair-washing ritual. With one eye on the clock and the other on Winnie-the-Pooh, I performed the story hour obligations. After a quick little "talk to Jesus" for each and a hasty good-night kiss, I turned out their lights and closed their doors. A few last-minute words of instruction to the baby-sitter and we were off. Nothing unusual.

The January evening was typical for Chicago—cold, icy, and snowy—no hint of crisis. Mark drove with extra caution. "Can't be too careful with this ice," he observed. He was right, of course, but I didn't give it much thought. Long ago I had gotten over routine fears. Icy roads didn't bother me. As a matter of fact, there wasn't a lot that really did bother me when it came to fears. I often threw caution to the wind and proceeded at my own pace, which was usually breakneck speed.

I was confident enough not to be bothered by fears, and at times was unsympathetic to those who were. "You can't let your fear paralyze you," I would glibly spout off if someone confided in me. I knew little about fear as I rang the doorbell and joined the party that cold January night.

The warmth and happiness of the evening made the time slip quickly away. The group around me was a happy one, and I felt very much at home in the crowd. They were my people. They were the ones with whom I had laughed and cried my way through college. I was relaxed. I was contented. As I rambled back over the past ten years, I appreciated more than ever God's good gifts to me.

Many of us hadn't seen each other since college, so the dinner party chatter included reminisces about every major and minor event of our lives for the ten years since we had all been together. Everyone was talking at once. We had so much catching up to do. Pictures to pass around, stories about our children to compare, and "remember when" jokes to laugh about. No one could stop talking. But suddenly they did. The chatter stopped. Words were left hanging in midair. And I was trying desperately to hang on to my life.

The interruption came without warning. My words stuck in my throat, halted by a piece of chocolate brownie. I opened my mouth. Nothing came out—not even a cough. I frantically reached for Mark. No words. No breath. Nothing except that frantic grab. The conversation faded. The room dimmed. Nothing . . . except desperate efforts to gasp. But there were no gasps, only a lifetime of seconds. Then strong arms grabbed me around my waist and strong hands pushed inward.

The evening was suddenly silent. My coffee was cold

and the culprit brownie lay half eaten on my plate. The room was so quiet all I could hear was my own breathing. Everyone else seemed to be listening for that sound too. It was there, but it was weak and tired. The party ended. Gentle hands helped me to the car and home.

The physical trauma of those breathless moments wore off after a night of deep, uninterrupted sleep. But the emotional trauma did not. I sat down to eat the breakfast Mark prepared for me. I could not eat. My throat tightened. My head started to spin. I could feel my heart pounding. I had to excuse myself from the table.

I continued to be plagued with a paralyzing fear. What if it happened when no one was around? What if it happened in front of the children? Whenever I thought about Saturday night, I would feel my heart starting to race and my throat starting to tighten. All my neat little theories about mind-over-matter went out the window. I felt fear. It was physical fear. My confident self-control was gone. Fear was controlling me. I was helpless.

The paralysis of fear was as draining for me as were those few breathless seconds. The day of fear extended into two days and then three. Each meal, no matter how tempting, became a battleground of mind over stomach. Each day became an effort to keep my mind from reliving the whole paralyzing scene. A chocolate brownie had become the ruler of my life.

In desperation, I searched my file for the folder stuffed with newspaper clippings about safety and first aid. I found an article I remembered reading a year ago about a hug that had saved many lives from a choking death. Somehow Mark too had remembered the article. I felt those lines of print. As I read, I could feel the familiar pounding of my heart and tightening of my throat.

The article told how to help someone who was

choking. I copied the suggestions on a three-by-five card and taped it to my most conspicuous kitchen cabinet door, right next to the list of emergency phone numbers. Then I stood in front of the bathroom mirror and, with newspaper clipping in front of me, rehearsed exactly what I would do if I choked while I was alone. My fears continued.

In the midst of my agonizing battle, I remembered a promise of liberation from God: "God did not give us a spirit of timidity but a spirit of power and love and self-control" (2 Timothy 1:7 RSV). If this battle were going to be won, I suddenly realized, God needed my cooperation. I described my fears to God just as I had to Mark.

And then I ate brownies. I purposely went out and bought the nuttiest chocolate brownies I could find. I ate four at one time. Each swallow was traumatic. My heart still pounded and my stomach violently rebelled against the chocolate offering. But I ate the brownies.

My excuses at mealtime stopped. I glued myself to my chair until I had eaten every bite. Before each meal, my silent conversation to God became, "God, You have not given me this spirit of fear, so it must be my own doing. You have given me power and self-control. Therefore, I will eat this meal in peace."

And I did. Before the week was over, Saturday night was a vague memory that evoked little emotion. I remembered the dinner. I remembered the noisy conversations and the happy reminiscing. I even remembered how good the chocolate brownies had tasted. Now, many months removed from that January night, I remember the monster of fear that held me in its grip, and I thank the Lord for the freedom to eat chocolate brownies and to truly enjoy them. It was as though in those few terrifying moments of silence I had lived a lifetime. Never again would I take so lightly the agonizing reality of fear.

The Cardboard Window

The thick gray smog that hung overhead matched the gray mood I felt as we drove through Chicago's west side ghetto. Even though the calendar said spring, the day was bleak and cold. The remainders of a recent snow storm lay in black, ugly heaps along curbs and streets. Trickles from melting black snow moved bits of debris and litter toward street gutters. Slush and dirt were everywhere. I unconsciously pulled my white spring coat closer, as though to keep the city from touching me.

People too were everywhere. Small, innocent faces appeared beside newspaper shacks on street corners. "Newspapers," they called weakly with equally small voices. Boys with clothes many sizes too big leaped over fire hydrants and scooted down narrow muddy alleys in search of excitement. A gang of girls with black leather jackets stood in a huddle along a curb and glared at us when we stopped at a red light. Men with empty faces leaned against dimly lit barber shops and cluttered laundromats. Mothers coming home from work got off buses and stopped at the corner grocery store to buy food for the evening meal.

We had just entered the land of the Latin Counts. Signs and symbols scrawled on the sides of buildings proclaimed their domain. A gang meeting was being held in front of one deserted garage. A few inattentive members played hockey in the street. As we slowed to avoid their game, I reached across and locked the door on my side of the car.

I shifted my eyes from the people. School buildings with broken windows and barred doors, tiny concrete playgrounds, dingy store-front churches, row after row of apartment houses with sagging wooden stairs and cardboard in place of window panes—all blurred together for me. I suddenly felt very tired and weary.

At last we saw our destination, a tiny store-front mission. It was almost dark, and the light from the third-floor apartment of our friends beckoned a warm welcome. We securely locked our car, and I tightened my hold on my purse as we tried to avoid puddles of melting snow and sidewalk debris. Past the delicatessen, up three flights of stairs, and through the open door of the home of our host and hostess for the evening. I relaxed as the door closed behind us.

The evening passed quickly and pleasantly. All was warm and secure and comfortable. We were three flights above it all.

As the clock struck ten, my thoughts turned toward home—home with its wide, tree-lined streets, landscaped lawns, and neat, well-kept homes. At home I could walk down the street and relax. At home I felt safe and secure.

Some families in our neighborhood were poorer than ours, some very poor, but the teenagers did not haunt the streets in tight-lipped groups, and the city street department kept streets and sidewalks clean.

At home were no broken windows or cardboard replacements, no boarded up store fronts or barred doors. At home, mothers went to the supermarket in taxicabs or in the family's second car. On the Northwestern express train, well-dressed fathers returned from a day of business in the Loop, careful to leave their boots and the city's dirt outside. At home there were swimming pools, tennis courts, and golf courses. At home there were million-dollar churches and clean, modern schools with football fields, stadiums, and fieldhouses. Yes, it was time to go home.

I kept my eyes closed most of the way home—perhaps because I was tired, perhaps because I wanted to forget, perhaps because I didn't want to be reminded of the difference. I was especially glad to be going home. I opened my eyes as the car slowed down and we turned the last corner. I loved the evergreen trees that framed our little home. They looked almost enchanted with a light layer of snow covering their branches. On the window ledge of our large living room window I could see my prized collection of crystal goblets that I had collected on our travels. The antique lamp above the kitchen table glowed a warm welcome as we pulled in the driveway beside our second car. Yes, it was good to be home.

The crunch of glass under my feet as I stepped through the door told me something was wrong. My heart sank as I looked around the kitchen. Shattered glass was everywhere. The curtains at the front window billowed freely in the night air. Pieces of white sink enamel lay scattered amid the glass. On the counter next to the sink lay a large, jagged rock. A gust of cold air snapped the torn curtains, giving me a brief glimpse down the street. In that silent moment I saw a long, long way. And when I looked at the piece of cardboard that replaced our shattered window the next morning, I saw even further. God's peace can walk the city streets, and sometimes violence comes to the suburbs. It took a cardboard window pane to help me learn.

Listen to the interruptions in your life.
What do you hear?

CHAPTER FIVE

Independence

A Man Went Free

A man went free the day You died.
  Barabbas.
    Hero.
    Macho Man.
    The People's Choice.
They cut his chains and
  buried his past
  in his empty prison cell.
Murder. Insurrection.
It didn't matter.

But they nailed You down,
Strapped You with the weight of a cross,
While he walked away clean.
They restored his dignity to him:
  Free man.
  Pardoned.
  No more labels.
But they stripped You,
Gave You thorns for Your crown.

A weed for Your scepter
And an obituary that read:
JESUS, KING OF THE JEWS.

They shouted his name through the city.
Blazed it in neon lights
    and put a marquee around it
While they drove You to the place
    of the Skull,
Gave You vinegar to drink,
    and threw dice for Your clothing.
When darkness came,
You bowed Your head
  and died
    alone
While he celebrated in the streets
    with the Passover crowd.

A man went free the day You died.
I was that man.

Struggle Under the Sink

The noise under the kitchen sink was horrendous. Most of the commotion was mechanical, but some of it was human—my own grunts and groans—as I wrestled with the wrench I thought would unjam the garbage disposal.

Mark *had* to have heard! He wasn't deaf. Most of the clatter I was making was for his benefit. But there he sat, upstairs at his desk preparing his class lecture, totally oblivious to my struggles under the sink.

After several intense but unsuccessful attempts to play plumber, I was convinced my pounding head would be forever tilted at a ninety-degree angle. The red, angry imprint of the wrench branded the palm of my hand. Admitting defeat, I finally swallowed my pride, held my aching head, and called for Mark.

"I have been working on this stubborn garbage disposal half the morning. My head hurts and my hand will never be the same. Would you *please* see what you can do?"

"Why didn't you call me sooner?" he asked. "There's a little red button at the back that you have to reset before it will work."

This time I knew he heard my groan. His response was a gentle rebuke. "I'm sorry, Honey, but I can't read your mind. I didn't know you needed help. I didn't even hear you down here. Next time, ask me before you get yourself all bent out of shape. Here, let me show you where the button is."

I thought a lot about our garbage disposal episode that day, and I came to the conclusion that many of the breakdowns in marriages probably come because husbands and wives fail to make their needs known to one another. We expect that our loving, sensitive, insightful partners will automatically anticipate our needs, read our thoughts, and accurately interpret all our nonverbal clues.

"Ask and it will be given to you. . . . For everyone who asks receives. . . ." Jesus said one day to his followers (Matt. 7:7–8). Jesus not only *talked* about communicating needs. He *did* it. He asked for a boat when He needed the privacy of the other side of the lake. He asked for a colt when He needed transportation into Jerusalem. He requested the presence of His three closest friends when He faced the grief of Gethsemane.

Scripture teaches need-stating. It's called prayer. If the infinite God of the universe, who knows all my thoughts, wants me to make my requests known to Him, how much more should I be willing to state my needs to my finite husband—to whom the capacity of mind reading has not been given!

Learning Life's Lessons

"Mom, I need new shoes," Nicky announced as he burst through the door after school. "Miss Bell says it's dangerous to run in gym with my toe sticking out."

I looked down at my son's blue tennies. Hadn't I just bought them last month? But the protruding toe, a slit along the side, and tattered laces told me he'd had them longer. "You're right, Nicky. It's time for some new tennies, but you'll have to wait until our next paycheck."

To a seven-year-old, two weeks is an eternity. "But I may break my toe by then," he pleaded. "I need them *now*."

"Sometimes life's lessons are hard to learn, Nicky. Seldom do we get what we want the minute we want it. Here is a chance for you to learn to get along with what you have until we have the money."

"But, Mother," Nicky protested, "I can't wear these shoes for gym anymore. Miss Bell said!"

I launched into an elaborate discourse on budgeting principles. "So you see, Nicky," I concluded, "that's how Mommy and Daddy spend money. Tennis shoes are not in the budget this time; next time they will be."

"Then I'll pray about my shoes," Nicky announced. "I'll tell God I need the money by tomorrow."

My mind did a panic-alert. How could I tell my son that God is not a giant mail-order catalog in the sky? How could I temper his impetuous request with "Thy will be done," when he had already decided what was to be done?

I swallowed hard. "OK, Nicky. Why don't you tell God about your need." Later, when he learned for himself that God does not issue cash on demand, I would explain to him about prayer.

When he left for school the next morning, new tennis shoes were still uppermost on his mind. "Can we buy my shoes tonight? You'll get the money today, because I prayed about it."

"We'll see, Nicky," I replied as I kissed him good-bye. There wasn't time to explain just then.

But the need to explain didn't come; Nicky's answer came instead. "This is long overdue . . . sorry for the oversight," said the note I received in the mail that afternoon. The enclosed check, payment for an article I'd written long ago and forgotten, was more than enough to pay for Nicky's new shoes.

After school, Nicky's blue eyes danced. "See, Mom I told you it would come. Now can we buy my shoes?"

Today Nicky wears new blue-and-gold tennis shoes— poignant reminders of a child's simple trust and of my need to continually relearn what faith is all about.

When the Ropes Come Down

Ropes in a swimming pool can be a nuisance. The bright yellow bobbers strung along the ropes look festive—like Japanese lanterns at an evening patio picnic—but who needs Japanese lanterns while swimming? They take up valuable space. Three bobbers in a row equals the width of one body. Someone always has to wait in the whirlpool because bobbers instead of people are floating in the lanes.

My suggestion? Keep the ropes out of the pool so more people can swim free and relaxed and without the fear of strangling themselves on a two-inch nylon cord. No boundaries. No worries about crossing over into someone else's lane. The whole pool is my lane.

One day our aquatics director got smart and took down the ropes for the early bird swim. Suddenly the pool was twice as wide, the bodies twice as many. Creative water works. We could swim free style. Chart our own course. Navigate circles, diagonals, diamonds, cubicles, if we wanted. Straight lines got old quickly. For thirty minutes I swam "free."

But in those thirty minutes, I was clobbered on the head by what felt like a two-hundred-pound butterfly stroke, gouged by a frog kick that violated my space, and asked politely if I would please swim next to the wall because I kept crossing into the next lane.

I climbed out of the pool feeling tense and irritable. The nerve of that woman to say I crossed her lane when there weren't even any lanes to cross. My head was still thumping from the muscular butterfly flap. Usually I went home from a swim feeling every muscle in my body had been massaged by the gentle waters. Today I was tied in knots, and my swimming skills had definitely deteriorated. My time was way up, my strokes uneven, and my breathing irregular.

Today our aquatics director was even smarter. He put the ropes back up. The 6 A.M. swim was surprisingly more pleasant for everyone. I still would prefer smaller yellow bobbers, but the boundaries? God knows how much better life works when we learn to live within them. I wonder why it takes me so long to learn.

Flying Solo

Overhead a flock of Canada geese spread across the October sky with the order and precision of a squadron of planes flying in formation. As I watched the V-shaped phenomenon honking its way southward, I was reminded of dependency. These nine-pound Canada geese—each measuring three feet in length and cruising thousands of feet in the air at speeds up to sixty miles per hour—may seem to be on their own. But their migratory feats do not depend on individual prowess.

Their secret of long-distance endurance flight is found in their ability to fly in *formation*. Directly behind one bird and in front of the other, each rides the powerful updraft created by its predecessor, depending on another for protection from battering headwinds. Flying solo is not God's plan for Canada geese flying south.

Neither is "flying solo" God's plan for the Christian,

though we sometimes act as if it is. We've been taught to be resilient, independent, strong. Rugged individualism is the "American way." To show that I need another is to show weakness. To lean on someone else means I am deficient. To allow another person to help means I am incapable of helping myself.

So I often fly solo. I try to "tough it out." And too often, ignoring my need for fellow Christians, I fly headlong into battering headwinds.

Evidently the Christians in Corinth had the same tendency because Paul felt it was necessary to write to them concerning their need for one another. According to Paul, we are one body, but many parts. Comparing individuals to parts of the body, he says, "And the eye cannot say to the hand, 'I have no need of you'; or again the head to the feet, 'I have no need of you'" (1 Cor. 12:21 NASB). The parts *need* each other.

What does it mean to need one another? If I need you, I will lay aside my "superwoman" image and let you know that I sometimes feel lonely, that at times I need a call from a friend—someone who knows and loves me and can be a "mirror" to silently reflect my inconsistencies.

Needing another means I won't have to do *all* the serving. It means that when my car breaks down I will allow you to lend me yours. When insecurities hit I will ask you to pray for me. When I feel overwhelmed I will allow you to offer me advice.

Who am I to think I don't need you? Watching that flock of Canada geese fly overhead reminds me that I do!

Listen to the independence in your life.
What do you hear?

CHAPTER SIX

Unearned Love

Splintered Wood

What is this cross I have to bear,
This splintered wood
That rubs against my flesh
Like a strip of coarse sandpaper?
This cross—
This dull, dead weight
That bends my spirits,
Pins hope to the ground?

I stumble along cobbled streets
On my way to my own Golgotha—
The "place of a skull."
I've walked these streets before;
When children skipped,
And old men sang
And young men
Watched the skies with hope.

But shadows fell across those skies.
Now old men mourn.
The children cry.
And the splintered wood
leans heavy on my back.
Darkness drops
Into the middle of the day.
The earth vibrates.
The ground shakes.
It's never been this way before.
Nature's flow erupts like a geyser.
And all around is turmoil.

I reach the city gate.
It is cold outside.
What is this hill I have to climb—
This place of barren rock
and dead-men's bones?
I clutch my cross
and stagger upward in the dark.
There is no other way around.
The wood tears deep into my skin.
Does no one understand my load?
Does no one know
the agony of lonely hills?

But on the stony skull ahead
I see another cross;
Rising out of the shadows,
Silhouetted against the dark.
"This hill," He said,
"Is one that you must climb.
This darkness you must feel.
But your cross—
the one that straps you
with its weight,
I carried once,
Up this same hill
For you
So that today, My child,
you may lay it down
And be free."

A Father's Gift

The storm clouds were gathering inside the car as well as out. Large, wet drops splashed against our windshield as we left church and started for home.

The outer turbulence, however, was easier to cope with than the inner. Our seven-year-old wore the storm on her face, flashed it in her eyes. Absolutely nothing was right in the back seat. Nicky had his foot over the middle hump, much too close to her semi-new sandals. The breeze from Mom's window was too cold, and the way Daddy dodged the road repairs was giving her a stomach ache.

There was nothing very positive to be said about her actions either. She smacked her gum, snapped at her brother, and sucked in her breath for special effect every time her daddy hit a bump in the road. All in all, the tempest in the back seat was something I chose not to tolerate. I opened my mouth to pronounce judgment, but Mark was there first.

"Jori. Nothing is going right for you today, is it? You are usually so positive. I want you to know that I love you." He slowed the car, turned around and smiled at her, choosing at that moment to not dwell on her actions but to affirm her character.

Her defenses crumbled. The storm subsided. The rest of the ride was peaceful. Spoken words of love and praise had overcome the turmoil.

In the Old Testament, the father, as God's representative of the home, conferred blessings upon his children. While the word "bless" in Scripture often means "to declare happy," the same Hebrew word "barak" and the Greek "eulogeo," may also be translated "to speak well of" or "to praise." We don't generally think of stormy rides home from church as a time to bless (praise or speak well of) our children, but I'm convinced that on that day, Mark gave Jori a gift she will use for years to come. By praising her, he taught her to praise others.

"If there be any praise," Paul says in Philippians 4:8 (KJV), "think [dwell] on these things." What better place to start dwelling on praise than with our children—even in the midst of storms.

Under No Conditions

"I love you," I said to a spotless face. No blueberry jam. No milk mustache. Each strand of hair in its proper place. "I've signed your report card. It's lying on the counter so you won't forget it. I'm proud of all those A's. Mrs. Harmon should be proud too."

I gave him an extra hug before he raced out and hopped on his red ten-speed. It glistened as much as his face that morning. "Your bike looks so clean. You must have worked hard to make it shine so much."

He waved good-bye, his new blue jacket billowing behind him. He looked handsome. The gray in his plaid shirt perfectly highlighted the blue-gray of his twinkling eyes. He had even chosen the right pants. Gray cords with a blue and gray striped belt.

"Yes, I do love that little guy," I said to myself as I turned to the morning clutter. Even his blue cereal bowl and plate were rinsed and stacked neatly in the dishwasher. So easy to love him when he's doing things right.

That was yesterday. Today he wants to help me in the kitchen. He has on dirty football pants, the ones with a big rip in the knee, and the old yellow football jersey that I had hid in his bottom drawer. It has stretched so much it is several sizes too big, and besides, yellow makes him look jaundiced.

He volunteers to help unload the groceries. As he climbs onto the countertop—football pants and all—the flour falls off the shelf, shattering my glass coffeepot in a thousand pieces. The can of frozen orange juice, intended for the freezer, misses its mark and hits my foot instead.

"Sorry, Mom. Didn't mean to do it."

I massage my little toe. "It hurts just as bad either way, you know." He doesn't seem to know.

Dinner is next on the agenda. My volunteer hangs around, and I put him in charge of the spaghetti. The water begins to boil, but the noodles slide out of the wrong end of the box as he carries it to the stove. He heads for the broom again.

"Out. Please. Out of the kitchen." His shoulders slump as he walks out the back door.

Then I think of the One who loves me when my face is dirty, hugs me when I've broken more than coffeepots, keeps His arms around me even when I've caused Him pain.

I go to the picnic table where Nicky sits with his head down. I encircle him in my arms.

"Honey, I love you." That was all I needed to say. His arms went around me and his dirty cheek rested against mine.

"Lord, keep me giving him hugs, especially when I think he least deserves them. Because that's what you do for me."

Rocks Don't Cry

Fathers don't cry.
They are
  Brave and strong,
  Steadfast and sure,
  Like a rock that never moves.
No time for tears,
Too controlled to cry.
Their world is concrete and asphalt,
Logic and logistics.
Rocks don't cry.
Neither do dads.

But you cried that day, Dad.
You wept for my rebelliousness.
Like the Father over Jerusalem,
You waited on the front porch for me,
Long after the lights were off.
You waited and wondered
While I
  Made my own choices,
  Ignored the fences,

And then came home hoping you didn't know.
  But you did.
Your tears washed over my rebellion,
Softened my will.
And I knew I was loved.

Rocks don't cry.
Neither do dads.
But you did that day.
You wept over my pain.
Like the man from Galilee who cried
  at His friend's grave,
You watched
  as the blood squirted from my vein,
Threatening a pipeline to life.
You held my hand
as the doctor sutured the skin
  ripped by a fall on broken glass.
You felt my groans.
And afterward I saw your tears,
Trickles of tenderness.
Your tears washed over my hurt,
And I knew I was loved.

Rocks don't cry.
Neither do dads.
But you cried that day.
You wept over separation.
  Like the One who cried in the garden,
You wiped your eyes with your big white handkerchief
Unashamedly
In front of all my friends
As the big white ocean liner
Pulled away from the dock
For seven days and 3,000 miles of
  Atlantic Ocean.
You were the only dad who came;
Rode the Greyhound bus for 12 hours
just to wave good-bye
And cry.
Your tears washed over the miles between us.

UNEARNED LOVE

Your big white handkerchief
Brought us together,
Held us together,
And I knew I was loved.
For in those tears
I saw strength.
My rock,
My Dad,
Who knew how to cry.

Listen to the unearned love in your life.
What do you hear?

CHAPTER SEVEN

Gains and Losses

Of Kingdoms and Crosses

I love you John, Peter, James, Andrew.
Here, let me offer you a kingdom.
First-vice president
Joint chief of staff
Right-hand man.
See that door?
We'll write our name in gold upon it.
See that mountain?
We'll build our tabernacle in the clouds.
One for you
One for me
And one for Elijah.
See those crowds?
We'll autograph our books
Sign them up for seminars
Put them on our mailing list.
I love you John.
Here's your three-piece-double-breasted suit
Your credit card
And your personal copy of
　　How to Win Friends and Influence People.

I love you Peter.
Here, let me teach you how to preach.
Three points.
Illustrations.
And a closing line for the cameras.

I love you James.
Church salesman of the year.
Your territory is everything west of the Jordan.
Direct mail will do.
Here's your ad copy writer.

I love you Andrew.
Let me multiply your loaves and fishes.
Contests.
Concerts.
Creative worship.
Keep those buses rolling in.

But
He went to a cross and died.
Strange way to build a kingdom.
Strange way to say I love you.

Lost and Found

"Being lost is when you're meant to be somewhere you're not." My nine-year old's answer was so simple it was profound. I could tell he knew whereof he spoke. His drama had started several hours earlier—just about dusk.

"Where's Nick?" Mark asked as he pulled the Datsun into the garage and prepared to close the doors for the night.

"I haven't seen him for hours. I thought he was with you." My words sounded the alarm in my brain. I could read concern in Mark's usually calm voice. "He and Jerry rode up to the park about three. I told him to be home by four."

I phoned the neighborhood circuit. Nicky was in none of his usual spots. Jerry had come home at four, almost two hours earlier. The last he knew, Nick was riding his bike on the dirt mounds out behind the library—the ones closest to the reservoir.

Suddenly everything was out of sync. Terrifying visions formed in my mind as we jumped in the car and headed toward the reservoir.

Even the twilight, usually gentle for me, seemed sinister and threatening. Nick was somewhere out in those shadows. And he was the kind of guy who always came home.

The night cadences had already begun to rise from the creekbed that bordered the library. Mark chose the creek path and I turned west toward the reservoir.

"N-i-c-k-y . . ." my call bounced between the mounds of dirt.

By day the hills were a constant source of adventure for nine-year-old dirt-bike enthusiasts, but this evening they loomed like monsters, and the reservoir beyond yawned hungrily.

Where was he? I felt the empty wilderness around me and shivered in its silence.

Suddenly, out from a clump of dried grasses and cattails, a small voice said, "Here I am, Mom. I'm on my way home."

The mud-figure, adorned in a wet and soggy baseball shirt that stretched out from under a dirt-plastered jacket, moved slowly toward me. Nicky carried his musket—a $7.95 replica of those used in Revolutionary War days, a souvenir from Williamsburg, Virginia. A powderhorn he had made himself was slung across his shoulders.

"Trey and I were fighting the Redcoats . . . except I forgot what time it was."

My tears finished the story for him. In fact, the three of us huddled there in a cold little clump and cried tears of relief. It was the only punishment Nicky needed.

"Mom, I'm really sorry," he said later that night as he snuggled beside me for his bedtime story. "I like it better when I'm home with you and Dad."

I thought of the One who grieves over my wanderings; who pursues me when I am meant to be somewhere I am not. There is no peace in being lost, because I was created to be found.

"The Good Life"

Bankrupt! The word has a sinister ring. It was what happened to someone else's family business, never to yours. But this time "bankrupt" seemed to be plastered all over the walls that for four generations had held our family enterprise together.

"The plant is closed," my dad said over the phone. "Boarded up and barred. The bank owns it now."

His voice sounded tired. What does a sixty-two-year-old man say when his life's blood has just been clamped off?

A million thoughts jostled around in my mind. I had wanted so much more for my parents in their retirement years—more than frozen assets, a lost inheritance, and a boarded-up industrial complex.

Hadn't they lived through enough financial head-aches? Sacrificed more than enough to put their five children through school? Experienced more than their share of lean years? Why couldn't they enjoy a taste of "the good life?" If two people ever deserved it, my folks did.

I had wanted them to retire in comfort. Nothing extravagant. Just enough security to enjoy some extras that life had never afforded them—a trip to Ecuador to visit a missionary friend, Sunday dinners out, a new carpet for their upstairs bedroom.

This whole thing is like a car rolling downhill backward, I thought last week when we visited Mother and Dad. *Here they are, working harder than ever with less to show for it. Odds and ends of house-painting jobs. Long, hot hours and a few commission sales for a local monument company. Do-it-yourself projects. Canning and freezing to cut the cost of groceries.*

I wished I could reverse the trend, pay to have their leaky faucets fixed, buy them a new mattress, a new carpet for their upstairs bedroom, a year's supply of steaks.

"The only treasure you take to heaven with you is your children," Dad said one night as he looked proudly around the table at his children and grandchildren. He prayed with us, then left to visit a man who had lost an arm, three fingers, and both eyes in a dynamite accident. It was time for their weekly Bible study.

As I watched Dad disappear into the silent evening, I remembered what Jesus said on the subject: "Lay not up for yourselves treasures upon earth . . . but lay up . . . treasures in heaven" (Matt. 6:19-20 KJV). Then it dawned on me that my folks *were* enjoying the good life. Giving them a new carpet for their bedroom suddenly didn't seem so important after all—not when compared to their lifetime of contented service to others.

Blooms in the Desert

Nothing about her appearance indicated success. For thirty years she had lived alone in two tiny rooms of adobe brick in a remote Indian village. Working tirelessly in a dispensary that opened its doors around the clock to pain, sickness, and suffering, my missionary friend had had no time to pamper herself.

We sat on the bare concrete of her front porch, sucked on ice cubes that had cooled our lemonade, and munched peanut butter crackers. One hundred-and-two degree heat steamed from the sun-baked earth, melted the ice in our glasses, and rolled down our faces in trickles of perspiration. Her life's companion, a mangy, long-haired mutt, thumped his tail now and then against the shadow of the pinon pine. Nothing else moved. Civilization had wound down.

I looked across the field of yucca and sage to the

church. No steeple, only a squatty square of red clay topped by layers of thatch that came to a point in the middle.

We had gone last night into that clay cathedral to sing and pray. Evening vespers, Marjorie had called it. She'd pumped out "Amazing Grace" on the portable organ as though she were playing a Bach fugue on the 6,000 pipes of St. Paul's in London. Her white tennis shoes never paused on the pedals. Three delicate pink roses, an offering from her tiny, triangular rose garden that grew just outside her kitchen door, graced the rough-hewn altar plank. *Blooms in the desert* I thought as I breathed in the fragrance.

Not many had come to worship under the thatch. A handful of barefoot waifs, who looked as if they had neither washcloth nor mother, sat straight and quiet on the front row of the backless benches, their dark eyes shining, their hands folded reverently in their laps. Several men in straw sandals and white shirts led the service. Their wives sat on the opposite side of the aisle, holding squirming babies and smiling during the entire service. Marjorie moved unobtrusively from organ to front row and when the vespers ended she gave a personal benediction— a warm hug—to everyone present. I couldn't understand her words, but I understood the smiles of pleasure they produced. The barefoot waifs hung on to her skirt and the leaders never took their eyes from her as she spoke. No one had to lock the door as we left because there wasn't one. Marjorie folded up her organ and we carried it down the path toward home.

"Aren't they marvelous people?" she asked later as she mixed powdered milk and water for our bedtime snack. "The men who led tonight were little boys I've watched grow up. Daniel has even been to Bible school." She spoke with the pride of a mother, smiled with the glow of youth. I noticed how free her face was of lines, despite her fifty-some years. She served the powdered milk in crystal goblets and put another dish of peanut butter crackers before us. The evening ritual had the air of high-tea.

This was our final evening. Tomorrow we would begin a two-day trek back to paved roads and concrete bridges. But first we would cross 130 miles of nature's desolation. Marjorie and I sat on the bare cement of her porch, which by now had been cooled by the evening's chill, and looked west toward the Sierra Madres in the distance.

"It's such beautiful country here, we really don't need roses," Marjorie said. "But I plant them just the same." I looked again at the sage and the yucca growing amid swatches of brown. She had said "beautiful." There was no doubt she had meant it.

"No place in all the world has sunsets like this." She spoke with the conviction of one who for many years had been looking over sage brush and yucca and seeing nothing but splendid sunsets over the sierras.

"Contentment is natural wealth; luxury, artificial poverty," the Greek philosopher Socrates once said. I knew there in that silent, isolated hamlet of central Mexico that I had witnessed contentment first hand.

Simplicity Lost

"Joy to the world! The Lord is come."

I looked for joy as I window-shopped with the Christmas crowd at one of our city's most fashionable shopping centers. The store was a decorated menagerie of costly merchandise from all over the world, and the shoppers who dished out fifty- and one-hundred-dollar bills for holiday "trinkets" reflected tastes and styles as international as the merchandise they purchased.

I looked for joy in the Madison Avenue celebration, in the faces of people who could buy two-thousand-dollar jade rings from Shanghai or fifteen-hundred-dollar teakwood trays from Burma.

I looked for joy, but I saw worry lines etched deep across their foreheads. I saw staccato gazes focusing on things, not people. I heard blasts of cold and impatient words. Frantic steps. Push. Shove. Buy. "Joy to the world"?

The scene brought other faces to my mind—contrasting images of another time, another place. A damp, dark street in a littered corner of Mexico City. A *mercado* filled with chunks of hanging pork, crates of live chickens, buckets of beady-eyed fish. Sights and sounds of Christmas? Precious few *centavos* exchanged for an evening meal. Dirt and dark and hunger. The tiny frame of a woman wrapped in a shawl that was sizes too big, calling into the night to advertise the latest edition of the city's *periodico*. A baby asleep behind her on a pile of bundled newsprint.

I shuffled along behind people in a hurry going nowhere. But I smiled into relaxed faces and looked into tranquil eyes. People who saw strangers and took them in. We sometimes communicated without exchanging words.

I sensed simplicity in that dirty back-alley street of Mexico City. Spirits uncomplicated by things, untouched by greed, unaware of artificial needs induced by Madison Avenue propaganda. Contentment. Peace. Joy. In a dirty back-alley street of Mexico City.

At this Christmas season, I'm reminded of a star, a simple stable, a child asleep on a bundle of hay. I wonder how much of that simplicity we have lost in the ribbons, tinsel, and wrappings of Madison Avenue.

"Joy to the world! The Lord is come; let earth receive her King. . . ." Perhaps it's time we get back to the simplicity of Bethlehem—and *there* find our king, our reason for joy.

Contentment Is . . .

I heard the voice but couldn't see the person. She was on the other side of the locker, just coming in from her early morning swim. Her voice sounded like the morning itself—bright, cheerful, and full of life. At 6:15 in the morning, it would catch anyone's attention. I heard its affirming tone.

"Delores, I really appreciated the book you picked up for me last week. I know the library was out of your way. I haven't been able to put the book down. Solzhenitsyn is a great writer. I'm glad you suggested him to me."

"Good morning, Pat," she greeted another swimmer. For a moment the melodious voice was silent, then I heard it again. "Have you ever seen such a gorgeous day? I spied a pair of meadowlarks as I walked over this morning. Makes you glad you're alive, doesn't it?"

The voice was too good to be true. Who can be that

thankful at this time of the morning? Her voice had a note of refinement to it. Probably some rich woman who has nothing to do all day but sip tea on her veranda and read Solzhenitsyn. I suppose I could be cheerful at 6 A.M. if I could swim and read my way through the day. Probably even owns a cottage in the north woods.

I rounded the corner toward the showers and came face to face with the youthful voice. She was just packing her gear. Her yellow housekeeping uniform hung crisp and neat on her fiftyish frame. It was a uniform I'd seen before—along with mops, brooms, dust cloths, and buckets. An employee of the facility at which I swam. She flashed a smile my way, picked up her plastic K-Mart shopping bag, and hurried out the door, spreading "have a glorious day" benedictions as she went.

I still had the yellow uniform on my mind as I swam my laps and sank down among the foamy lather of the whirlpool. My two companions were deep in conversation. At least one of them was. His tired, sad voice told tragic woes of arthritic knees, a heart aneurysm, sleepless nights, and pain-filled days.

Nothing was good or right. The water was too hot, the whirlpool jets weren't strong enough for his stiff knees, and his doctors had been much too slow in diagnosing his case. With his diamond-studded hand, he wiped the white suds out of his face. He looked ancient, but I suspected he too was fiftyish.

The yellow uniform and the diamond studded ring stood out in striking, silent contrast, proof to me again that when God says "Godliness with contentment is great gain," He really means it. This morning I saw both contentment and discontent. I resolved never to forget.

In Comparison

Not every day does a former Miss USA walk into the room and take a seat three people from where I am sitting. The minute I saw her I knew she was no ordinary blue-eyed blonde. The sparkle in her eyes, the grace in her movements, and the confidence in her voice told me she was someone special.

She chatted comfortably with those who knew her and graciously included those of us who didn't. I was glad to be separated from her by three people, for I suddenly felt a striking contrast between Miss USA and me.

Her voice was smooth and mellow. Her perfectly manicured hands lay folded and relaxed on the table's edge. For the first time that evening I had nothing to say. My hands looked rough. My nail polish was chipped. I'd rushed out of the house without taking time to do a repair job. I hadn't noticed my hands before. And when I dressed for the evening, I felt okay about the dusty rose outfit I was wearing. Now, however, in contrast to the vibrant burgundy dress at the other end of the table, mine looked pale and outdated. Until now, the externals hadn't mattered.

By the time my evening with Miss USA was over, I had reduced myself to a second-class citizen. I hadn't traveled the world, spoken to hundreds, or won music scholarships. I had always thought *class* didn't matter. Tonight, I wasn't so sure.

"Ruth!" She reached out and touched my arm as we moved away from the table. Her smile seemed genuine. We stepped back from the group. "I've been wanting to meet you to tell you how God has used your gift to minister to me. Please keep writing for people like me who need it."

My game was over. I knew what I'd been playing. I'd been caught up so much in comparisons that I could not enjoy God's gift in someone else without feeling that it diminished *me.* I went home that evening feeling sad. *The game of comparing,* I thought, *is the root of much unhappiness and dissatisfaction.*

But games don't need to last a lifetime. Sometimes a brief encounter is enough to remind us of God's principles. "Each one should test his own actions. Then he can take pride in himself, without comparing himself to somebody else" (Gal. 6:4). Today that verse is written on an index card and taped above my kitchen sink as a silent reminder that who I am before God is all I have to offer. It is all He wants.

Listen to the gains and losses of your life.
What do you hear?

CHAPTER EIGHT

Tenderness

If I really cared . . .

If I really cared . . .
   I would look you in the eyes
     when you talk to me;
   I would think about what you are saying
     rather than what I am going to say next;
   I would hear your feelings
     as well as your words.

If I really cared . . .
   I would listen without defending;
   I would hear without deciding
     whether you are right or wrong;
   I would ask you why,
     not just how and when and where.

If I really cared . . .
   I would allow you inside of me;
   I would tell you my hopes,
     my dreams, my fears, my hurts;
   I would tell you when I've blown it
     and when I've made it.

If I really cared . . .
   I would laugh with you but not at you;
   I would talk with you and not to you;
   And I would know when it is time to do neither.

If I really cared . . .
   I wouldn't climb over your walls;
   I would hang around until you let me in the gate.
   I wouldn't unlock your secrets;
   I would wait until you handed me the key.

If I really cared . . .
   I would love you anyhow;
   But I would ask for the best that you can give
   And gently draw it from you.

If I really cared . . .
   I would put away my scripts,
   And leave my solutions at home.
   The performances would end.
   We'd be ourselves.

Kinder Words Were Never Spoken

I could tell the minute he walked in the door that it had been a long day. Even his eyes looked tired. I knew there was nothing I could do except take his briefcase and reach out to him with a hug.

I felt my own inner disarray, my physical and emotional fatigue. Sunrise to sunset activities had drained my reserve, and the day's demands were still far from over. Evening chores loomed above me like an impossible mountain: children to supervise; dinner to prepare for tomorrow's company; a house to clean; a lesson to plan for a morning class.

Now, standing before me, was my exhausted husband who had spent all his energy controlling his own twelve-hour day. His favorite easy chair stood waiting for him by the fireplace, the day's newspaper still folded nearby. *He deserves that chair, that fireplace, that paper*, I thought. *He's given more than his share. It's not his fault that the things on my list haven't gotten done.*

He hung his coat in the closet and exchanged his shoes for slippers. Then, rolling up his sleeves, he walked into the pumpkin-pie clutter of the kitchen.

"Been a long day." He yawned and stretched his arms wearily. Then, as though moved by some inner strength, he said, "Now, tell me what I can do for you."

His statement spread like a soothing ointment over the commotion of my day. I couldn't remember ever hearing kinder words. Not "Call me if you need me," or even "Let me know if I can do anything," but "What can I do for you?"—a genuine offer to help!

As I looked into Mark's tired but willing face, I saw a representation of the One who said He had "not come to be served, but to serve . . ." (Mark 10:45). Those words were spoken by the Son of God on a day when His disciples needed a proper perspective on servanthood (10:36) and when a blind man cried out for mercy (10:51).

The Son of God, surrounded by endless requests and wearied by miles of walking, looked *need* squarely in the face and asked, "What do you want Me to do for you?" No claim to His easy chair or thirty minutes with the daily paper by a peaceful fireside. Instead, He saw the burden another carried and offered to help with the load.

In a day when *servanthood* is dying for lack of examples and we get all tied up in theological knots over even the meaning of the word, we might do well to start where Jesus did—with a simple question, "What can I do for you?" Who knows? Those words might revolutionize our marriages as well as our relationships with our children and friends.

Once There Was a Good Samaritan

Once upon a time, in the spring of the year, when trees turn a feathery green and buds begin to force their way out of branches, a Samaritan traveled down a road from one city to another. She was a good Samaritan—warm and sensitive to the needs of others, always willing to come to the aid of someone who hurt.

It was not unusual, therefore, that when the Samaritan came upon a bruised and battered form lying beside the road, she stopped to offer assistance. She felt great sympathy for the wounded victim and gently took her to the nearest place of safety.

That night she listened for a long time to the sorrowful events of the bruised and battered. The Samaritan saw loneliness on her face, heard calls for help. She determined then and there that she would cancel her plans indefinitely in order to minister to the needs of the injured.

With great intensity she threw herself into the task of restoring the wounded. She listened, prayed, and encouraged. By and by, a strange thing began to take place.

Gradually, quietly, scenes from her patient's unfortunate life became so real in her mind that she began to feel the hurts herself. Night after night she went to bed exhausted, dreaming lonely dreams and hearing calls for help. Her resources were nearly drained, and she began to wonder why she saw so little progress in her patient. After all, she thought, I am faithfully bearing another's burdens, as the Lord of the kingdom commanded me to do.

One day when she felt she could bear the load no longer, the Lord of the kingdom passed her way and saw the strain on her body. "Put down the load, My child," He said. "I want you to carry one another's burdens, not absorb them. I alone am strong enough to do that."

The good Samaritan cried tears of relief. Realizing she could not, and was not expected to, carry forever another's load as well as her own, she returned to her patient. "I've given you what I can," she said. "Now I must move on."

The good Samaritan went on her way. But her thoughts return now and then to the wounded form found beside the road that spring day. Now, whenever she comes upon one who's fallen, she stops to lift that person up. But she does so without allowing the injured one's burden to cause her to stumble too.

I know. I was that good Samaritan.

Priority Mail

YOU COME TO ME
In words
Written on yellow sheets of
Notebook paper
Inked in blue
Folded and stuffed
In a plain, white envelope

Lots of letters
Come and go
In my post office box
But only one
Matters
The one that brings
You
To me

I know the writing
Tear open the seal
Time stops
Even people wait

There is just
You
  And me
And the letter

I find a place without people
A solitary spot under a birch tree
To read about
You
And me
And us

I belong to those words
To the one who penned
The neat block letters
I look for you behind the lines
Where are you as you write?
What are your feelings?
What are your thoughts?
What were you doing
Before you wrote?
What will you do
When you are done?

I look for meaning
I read between the lines
In search of
Your love
In search of
  The you that I love
I read again
The same words
But new information
Four times
Over the yellow pages
With blue block letters
And I've missed half of lunch
But nothing matters
Except
You are here with me
In words

TENDERNESS

Delivered in a twenty-cent envelope
That seems like gold

BUT IMAGINE:
An unopened letter
From the one
You love

IMAGINE:
Unread correspondence
From the God
You love

Thy King Cometh

Darkness settled in around me as our car coasted to a silent stop on the shoulder of the expressway. In a steady stream of purring motors and glowing headlights, Christmas Eve passed by us. All in a hurry. Off to a glad celebration of family and friends. Lights in the dark. A promise of hope. Only to fade into red glows disappearing down Interstate 55.

The warm splendor of city lights rising from the distant horizon made us even more aware of our dilemma. There were no lights in our car. They had died with the motor. Inside and out, all was cold, dark, and silent.

At least we were on the safe side of the city, where Cadillac Sevilles and Suburban station wagons moved in and out of the night. Soon one would stop to help us.

But all that stopped was a pickup truck that sounded like a piece of earth-moving equipment. It ground to a halt behind us. From the other side of the city, the wrong side. I reached over and locked both doors.

"Come on. We have a ride," Mark said. He helped me into the cab of the truck, which was little more than a heap of rust held together by two doors and a floor. Dust. Dirt. Bottles. Unkempt. Unclean. Heavy smell of alcohol.

Three hours later the couple still hovered over us like angels sent to guard. They followed the truck with our car in tow to the garage, hung around until the repairs were made, led us back onto the Interstate, then tooted their final farewell. And somewhere in the night two of a different kind went on about their business of Christmas Eve while we headed home to celebrate with family.

Thy King cometh. Not in Cadillac Sevilles or Suburban station wagons. But in drafty pick-up trucks that vibrate the earth when they move. Thy King cometh. In gold, frankincense, and myrrh, laid in the dust before deity's child. For the message of Christmas, the true message of Christmas, is that Majesty came, wrapped itself in swaddling clothes, and stabled itself in hay. Behold, thy King cometh unto thee.

Listen to the tender moments of your life.
What do you hear?

CHAPTER NINE

Commitments and Covenants

Human Dilemmas

No one wants to talk
They are lost in private cubicles
Mainliner magazine
Yellow notebook pads
Documents
Data
Seatbelts
And sometimes sleep.
Row 11. Seat E.
I settle in. In fact,
I don't want to talk either.
I'm glad the man next to me
Is reading The Wall Street Journal.
That way I don't have to tell him
Where I've been
Where I'm going
And what I do for a living.
Besides,
It's hard to talk
Against the roar of the engines.
Cubicles are easier. Safer.
Safer
Until the warning bell . . .
"Did he say 'the warning bell'?"
"Aborted take-off . . ."
The pilot has spoken.
The giant bird sits lifeless
At the end of the runway.
Engines silenced.
Someone say something.

Tell us it's okay.
How about another plane?
Another flight?
Another anything.
In our nervousness we wait.
And in our wait
We reach over the walls of silence
To find another human,
Someone else whose palms are sweaty,
Someone else who is thinking
Home
Family
And why did I ever choose this flight?
Suddenly words flow freely.
There are no strangers on this flight.
We are closed up together
In uncertainty—uncertainty that
Locks us in conversation
About where we've been
Where we'd like to go
And what we do for a living.
All the way to Minneapolis
We talk
Drawing support
For our faltering courage
Comfort for the
Uncertain sounds and the
Unusual take-off
Relief from
Warning bells
Fears
And isolated cubicles.

Human dilemmas—
They dissolve silence
And, if we let them
They draw us together
They draw us to the God
Who understands human dilemmas.

The Viking Cowboy

"When does a job become more important than the people you love?" As a Christian concerned about God's priorities for my life, I've often asked that question. In an unexpected way, I met my answer.

His ten-gallon hat barely cleared the doorway as he boarded Flight 721 in St. Louis. As he moved his towering frame down the aisle, swung his genuine cowhide case into the overhead compartment, and eased into the seat next to mine, I could tell this was no ordinary cowboy.

He was as cool and masculine as any aftershave commercial. He knew all the right lines and used them generously on everyone around him. I buried myself in my *Mainliner* magazine and tried not to notice. I wasn't enamored with a cowboy who appeared to have an ego twice the size of his hat. And I wasn't about to fall for his act.

"That a good article?" his voice boomed in my direction.

"Uh-huh."

"Ever heard of the Minnesota Vikings? I play football for them."

Something in his tone sounded haunting. I sensed there was more he wanted to say. I closed my magazine and listened. He glanced across the aisle, then back at me. No one was watching. He quit acting.

"Golden boy. Down the tubes." As he motioned thumbs down, I noticed his ring with an NFL insignia.

"See these eyes? They're red from crying. Just left my wife and two sons. Can't even be with them anymore. Kicked out of my own house. Didn't know football players cried, did you?"

As the 727 roared toward Chicago, he spilled out the pieces of his broken dream. Hard work. Irregular schedules. Frequent moves. Always the excuse that someday they would have time for each other. But one day there was no more someday.

"You know what my job became?" he asked. "An ego trip, that's what! After a while, my job was everything. Couldn't even hear what my family was saying.

"You write articles. Tell your readers that when a job makes you deaf to your family, you'd better *quit*. Tell 'em I said so—and I ought to know!"

We pulled up to the United gate, but even the congestion on Concourse E didn't interrupt the cowboy's discourse. "You've got your family," he exclaimed. "Hang on to them for all you're worth. Make them feel they're the most important thing to you. It's an empty world without them. I ought to know."

He tipped his ten-gallon hat in my direction, and I watched him climb into his waiting limousine and head for downtown Chicago. *Tomorrow,* I thought, *he'll be back running touchdowns.*

"Tell your readers," he'd said to me, "when your job makes you deaf to your family, you'd better quit." I promised him I would.

Partners in Covenant

I could tell by the way she twirled her wedding ring and tapped her coffee mug with her spoon that she had something important on her mind.

"Well, Ruth," she began, "our love is dead. There's nothing there anymore. After ten years of being married to him, about all I feel is that I have a *friend*. I can't go on living with a man I don't love."

Her words did not surprise me. Her happiness had vanished like the last rays of a setting sun. I knew she was contemplating divorce. *Why remain married when love has died?*

Since that talk with Amy, I've thought long and hard about love and marriage and have decided that marriage is not only a matter of love but of will as well. My heart does not determine its success or failure; my head does. Oneness is a choice I make, not something I feel.

But I live in a world of sentimentality. The media clamors for my heart, not my head. It teaches me to feel, but not always to think. It paints happiness with sunsets and roses. Sells love in a red velvet valentine. Promises intimacy in a bottle from Paris. And when the sunsets fade and the rose petals fall, the forces around me say: "Look for other sunsets, other roses. There is no reason to continue . . ."

Except one—the covenant I made. A rational agreement. Not a conditional commitment that changes with circumstances. A promise to be kept whether or not the warm fuzzy feelings last.

Sometimes Mark forgets that I need the car on Wednesday. And sometimes he tracks mud or snow on my freshly waxed floor. But we are still *partners* in a covenant. I decide to love, to overlook, to forgive and forget. Not because these things come naturally for me, but because I know forgiving will make it easier for us to keep our promise to each other.

How well I remember when Mark and I bought our first house. We knew it was perfect for us and were convinced God had directed. Boldly we paid our earnest money, signed the contract, bound ourselves legally to that house. Our money had spoken.

But the aftermath was emotional. What if we'd made the wrong decision? What if things got tough and the money wasn't there? What if we found defects in the house? What if we outgrew it? What if another house would have been better?

We *could* back out—except we'd signed and sealed the agreement with cash. The investment was too high. The cost of pulling out was too great. There was no turning back. Our wills held us to the monetary commitment we had made.

Although buying a house is a far cry from a lifetime commitment to marriage, I suggest that if we have learned to honor commitments as temporary as buying a house, perhaps it's time we apply the principle to commitments as permanent as marriage.

To Have or To Hold?

"Want to know the two most important things parents can do for their teenagers?" asked a silver-haired father of four grown children. "Trust them and let them go. You remember that someday when you have teenagers."

He was a stranger to me—a casual conversationalist at a social event. But I had the feeling his advice was worth remembering; soon I would be the parent of a teenager.

Today I read about a parent from a different time and place and recalled the advice of the silver-haired stranger.

In response to Pharoah's edict, "No more Hebrew boy babies!" this mother tried a daring plan. A basket lined with tar and pitch, papyrus reeds as camouflage, the waters of the mighty Nile, her baby son—and the daughter she trusted.

This Hebrew mother knew that supervising a dramatic

escape was adult business. It called for quick thinking, wise action, and stable emotions. She understood the perils her daughter would face, but she trusted her daughter and she trusted God.

After placing her son in the basket, she deposited it among the reeds and stationed her daughter beside the river on standby alert. Then she went home to attend her duties of the day, leaving the fate of baby Moses with Miriam, a young girl about the age of my twelve-year-old Jori.

As Jori grows older I hope I will remember the young Hebrew girl whose mother had enough confidence in her to trust her to make life-and-death decisions for her infant brother. With that kind of affirmation from a parent, it is little wonder that Miriam grew up to be one of Israel's great leaders.

"Trust them and let them go," the stranger advised. And in his advice I discovered another of God's amazing paradoxes. To keep your teenagers, you must let them go.

Nicky unknowingly illustrated the truth one day while blowing soap bubbles in the backyard.

"Don't try to hold on to the bubbles," Nicky directed his guests in typical eight-year-old fashion. "That's how they go away."

He balanced a colorful giant bubble in the palm of his hand to demonstrate. The delicate sphere swayed gently with the breeze, but remained securely in his hand.

"See," he explained, closing his fingers, "if you try to grab it, you lose it."

And the bubble was gone.

In the silent explosion of Nicky's soap bubble the stranger's advice regarding children came back to me: "Trust them—and let them go."

Easy Commitment

Commitment was always an abstract term to me until I saw it demonstrated one day at an airport in Colombia, South America.

At 9:00 A.M. steam was already rising from the parched red clay. As we drove through the gate toward the concrete square that seemed to squat in the middle of nowhere, we realized this was no ordinary day at the Cúcuta airport. Lines of green school buses clogged the parking area, and the entire town seemed to be moving *en masse* toward the terminal. Not a suitcase was in sight.

The activities at the Cúcuta airport that day appeared to have nothing whatever to do with travel. For those of us trying to go somewhere, a seven-hour wait began.

We threaded our way through the human barricades of green army fatigues, pushed past bayonets and billy clubs, and asked if there was a plane going to Miami.

"*El presidente* is coming," was the response we got. "No planes." Bands played, people yelled, banners fluttered. Everyone seemed caught up in the excitement, but not everyone in the crowd was cordial.

"Dissidents," we were told, as we watched the angry mob from behind the safety of glass doors. "Angry at their poverty. They want *el presidente* to know."

That day I saw a living demonstration of commitment. A young woman dissident held the restless crowd in her power as she waved a red flag. Her dark eyes blazed, and her long hair switched wildly as she oscillated from place to place like a fan on high speed. The sun poured down its 104-degree rays, and the air was motionless.

Inside the terminal we munched our sandwiches and drank ice cold Cokes. Outside, in the broiling noon-day heat, stood the woman of commitment. No lunch break or shade for her. Sweat ran down her face as she pounded the air with her fists. Her audience cheered.

Seven hours later her mission was accomplished. Her *presidente* had heard. The military pushed the all-day demonstration back into the waiting buses, and once again the Cúcuta airport became a place of transportation.

As we lifted off that clay oven, still steaming at four o'clock in the afternoon, I thought of how much my commitment to Christ costs me. A commitment served on padded pews in an air-conditioned sanctuary with people I enjoy seeing once a week! Can I even call it commitment if it doesn't cost me something?

Listen to the commitments and covenants in your life. What do you hear?

CHAPTER TEN

Mountains and Monuments

Rooted

Life is full of forces,
Forces that make me like a blade of grass—
   dried
   detached
   carried along by a breeze.
   Its direction depends on the wind.
   It rests for awhile
   until the next gust comes along
   and carries it somewhere else;
   no direction
   no weight of its own
   completely at the mercy of
      outside forces.

God, I need inside force.
Give me whatever it takes
to make a tree stand:
the sap that makes it live
the roots that keep it anchored
no matter how hard the wind is blowing.

Show me the rivers
where I can put my roots down deep.
Give me the courage of a tree
And not just a blade of dried grass.

Some Thoughts on Monuments

Not even a whisper could be heard in the vast cathedral with its towering arches and translucent domes. A sacred silence hung over the marble pillars, draped the golden altar, and muted the velvet and mother-of-pearl.

In the middle of downtown Maracaibo, Venezuela, surrounded by dusty streets, fruit vendors, barking dogs, and painted stucco, man had created his altar of worship to God. I stood amazed at the ability to create so delicate a balance of order and beauty.

As I left the cathedral in Maracaibo that day, I thought of other altars—formal and informal—built as memorials to the visitation of God. Altars built by Noah, Abraham, Isaac, Jacob, and Moses. Pilgrims and strangers. People in transit. They had survival to think of, tents to pitch on the sandy desert floor, herds to tend, families to feed. Yet they built altars. Some were piles of rough, irregular stones and sod collected from the wilds. But each stone was laid with intricate precision and skill. Centuries later, some still remain on the plains of the Middle East.

I also thought of tabernacle altars, defined and specific, blue-printed by God. Acacia wood from the mimosa trees that grew along the Dead Sea. A tough and beautiful orange-and-brown-hued encasement. Overlays of brass, copper, and gold. Four horns and a crown. Prototypes of altars yet to come in Jerusalem—the temples of Solomon and Herod.

These altars, fifteen feet high and thirty feet across, were even more magnificent and impressive than their desert predecessors. The focal point, a tower of bronze surrounded by terraced stairs, represented man's approach to God.

We don't build Old Testament altars anymore. The tables of stone are replicas of the past. They have been replaced "by a new and living way opened for us through the curtain, that is, His body" (Heb. 10:20).

Our altars of worship have deteriorated into a few haphazard moments with God. No beauty. No pleasant fragrance. Just a kind of magical charm to ensure a peaceful day. We leave no monument—no permanent record that on this spot God has spoken. No memorial to His greatness, His love, His care. We leave no record, for often we have not heard His voice above our own chatter.

I think it might not be a bad idea if we'd learn to build altars again—daily, orderly, specific monuments to the fact that God has spoken. In doing so, we might relearn what it means to "worship the Lord in the beauty of holiness" (Psalm 29:2 KJV).

Stepping Out

It's like
  jumping into an icy mountain stream
    from dry, hot rocks;
  rolling out of a warm sleeping bag
    into a cold morning;
  turning the shower off
    and stepping out;
  going off the high dive
    for the first time;
  not reaching for another potato chip;
  typing the first word
    of the book you are writing;
  pushing yourself off a cliff
    because there is no other way down.
Trusting God is hard to do.

Blessed Are the Hungry

At first glance nothing about the stately old church appeared out of the ordinary. The white clapboard frame was obviously old, probably dating back to the mid-1800s. The steeple, like all other church steeples, stretched heavenward, pulling my thoughts with it . . . *An infinite God is up there who dwells not only in temples made by hand, but in the sanctuary of my heart.* It was a fortifying thought in the middle of my busy day of travel and meetings.

I pushed open the cast-iron gate and followed the fence around the buildings. Stained glass windows seemed almost lifelike. Figures of the God-Man Jesus. The Bread of Life. The Shepherd of the sheep. The Door. The Vine. The Living Water. The Resurrection and the Life.

Magnificent structure, I thought to myself. In my mind I complimented some pilgrim of the past who had constructed his altar to God.

My first hint that the inside of the structure didn't match the outside was the oak-carved pulpit in the vestibule. Instead of a Bible resting on the ornate fixture, I saw after-dinner mints, a reservation log, and a sign that read, "Welcome to the Sanctuary. Luncheon served: 11:30–2:30. Dinner: 5:00–10:30."

A wide aisle carpeted in red led to the altar. But beneath the majestic arches and gilded organ pipes stood a buffet table. Puffed Mushrooms. Fried Zucchini. Baked French Onion Soup. Julienne Salad. Brochette of Beef.

The organ cubicle had become a bar; the baptistry, a fish tank; and the pews, cozy conversation centers for four.

I surveyed the scene before me and pondered its implications. Houses of worship—the places where we once fed our souls—had been turned into fancy restaurants to fill our stomachs. Where once we came with an appetite for God, we now come with a craving for prime rib and filet mignon.

"Well, that will keep me filled 'til dinner," a jolly man said as he paid the hostess and struggled to button his vest.

I thought of Jesus' words, "Blessed are those who hunger and thirst for righteousness, for they shall be satisfied" (Matt. 5:6 NASB). I returned to my car feeling sad for a society whose need to eat has become more important than its need to worship God.

Christmas Burnout

The December day was brilliant but the mood that followed me up the church stairs was dark. I'd walked here many times before, but today it seemed I was treading on alien turf.

"Ruth, you won't believe it," was all the church secretary said to me as she unlocked the doors, flipped on the light switch, and waited for me to enter. I stared at the ruins before me.

"It all happened in about five hours," she said. "A policeman spotted the smoke about 5:30 in the morning . . ." She reached out and touched a window ledge where a glass hurricane lamp was baked dark brown and a white dove turned blackbird stood with his tail in the air and his head pointed down. "Our Christmas concerts were scheduled to begin on Saturday night. The sanctuary was all decorated."

I moved silently through the blackened shell. *My church doesn't live here anymore.* The thought was like a death knell. We had dedicated both our children under the giant wooden cross that had hung at the front of the sanctuary. Today there was no cross. Instead, massive organ pipes spread out over the choir loft like melted candles.

I walked to the platform where two-year-old Jori had said her first lines in a Sunday school Christmas program. A star had shone overhead and shepherds had walked down the center aisle while the organ played "O Little Town of Bethlehem." Today there was no music. Instead, broken glass and ashes crunched under our feet.

Christmas—swallowed up by a tragic fire. I turned to go, but a white cup among a tangled mass of melted plastic caught my eye. Its whiteness told me it had been placed there since the fire. As I moved closer I saw on it the red shield of the Salvation Army.

"They came early," the secretary said, "and stayed through the day, serving hot coffee and doughnuts, doing whatever they could. We didn't know them. But they came, just to show they cared, I guess."

As we closed the door on the cold, dark sanctuary, I knew that the message of Christmas had been preached from this place after all.

Long ago, the God of the universe came via Bethlehem to visit the charred ash heaps of life. Now I see Him in the lives of people who come to care for the burned out places of my life.

Listen to the mountains and monuments in your life.
What do you hear?

CHAPTER ELEVEN

Passing Time

Looking Back

We were together again.
This time we spent our morning over coffee and
quiche in a little French cafe on Broadway:
　　South America in review, current projects, life in Manhattan,
　　　　　　people we knew, where do we go from here?
We said good-bye until my next trip east.
I flew homeward but thought backward—
　　Did I talk too much? Say the right things?
　　Take the conversation only where I wanted it to go?
　　Unwrap more of myself to her than I should have?
　　Was I witty? Sincere? Interesting? Caring? Informed?
　　Will she invite me for brunch next time I'm in New York?
She was someone I liked. Respected. Admired.
It mattered what she thought.
Put the movie on the reel and run it through again. "Beautiful sky
　　we flew through, wasn't it?" He handed me my coat from the
　　overhead compartment. "I'm sure it was." But I really hadn't
　　noticed.

We didn't agree—my nine-year-old daughter and I.
"Everybody else's mother is letting them go . . .
I'll be the only one . . . the odd ball . . . always the odd ball."
Exchange of words: Thoughtful. Calm. Firm.
Discussion ended . . . then resurfaced,
This time to create waves—
Tidal waves that capsized any hopes for rational conversation.
She slammed the door. Off to school in the eye of the storm.
I moved on with my day but relived the storm.
　　Was I too harsh? Too narrow? Too protective?
　　Did I react rather than act? Push her too far?
　　Leave my fingerprints all over the image she had of herself?

Stuff her back inside her hide-away shell?
She was at a delicate age. Fragile ego.
Balancing on a precarious perch.
It mattered how I treated her.
Put the movie on the reel and run it through again.
    "What did you do today?" he asked as he sat his briefcase
        down in the front hall and gave me a hug. "Well, I
        . . . I thought a lot. Funny I should be so tired."

The performance had ended. Lights turned off.
They closed the door. I kept it open.
Instant replay of the scene.
   Was it too long? I forgot to set my watch.
   Enough illustrations? I wish I'd used another one.
   Left out point number three. Good point, too.
   Meant to say . . . I think it came out something else.
   Did I talk about what they feel? What do they feel?
   Should have asked more questions beforehand.
People judge you on your finished product . . .
Grade you on performance.
It matters how I do.
Put the movie on the reel and run it through again. "Enjoyed your
    talk. Learned a lot," The monogrammed notecard said.
    Strange she should feel that way about my failure.

Lord, when I say good-bye to friends,
Help me think about them and forget about me.

When I discipline my children,
Help me do what I need to do and spend the rest of the day on
    other things.

When I finish a talk,
Help me close the door and leave it behind.

Don't let me go through life facing backward.

When Old Is Young

Uncle Alton wasn't really all that young. In fact, he told me he was somewhere around ninety-two or ninety-three. But in some ways, Uncle Alton was the youngest man I ever knew.

He wasn't really my uncle, or anyone else's uncle except Christine's, but for miles around he was everybody's uncle. After I stopped by to visit him on that hot day in August, I knew why.

The minute I knocked on the wooden screen door, he appeared, shuffling toward me in his bright blue shirt and Osh-Kosh bib overalls. I'd never seen a spryer shuffle.

"Come in. Come in. S'glad to see ye. Glad to see ye." His eyes were wide sparkles of blue that matched his shirt. His mouth was on the verge of laughter. In fact, his whole face looked like laughter—a look that didn't fade even after I'd been there for an hour.

I had come to see Christine, but Uncle Alton automatically became my host. He asked how I was, set the oscillating fan in my direction, and quietly called Christine in from the kitchen.

His eyes never shifted into a stare, and he never went to sleep. He followed every word with great interest, nodding his head vigorously when he agreed or remembered the event we were discussing.

Uncle Alton was all color. When I asked about the past, he talked about it. He recreated the days of mule wagons as he told how he had run the muddy ruts of the road in front of the house. He told about the sugar caning he had done with a team of horses harnessed to a revolving log that served as a press. But he seemed much more interested in the present—in the patch of watermelons he was watching over, in the deep purple hydrangea that was blooming just outside his window, or in the tiny humming-birds he fed each morning. He teased Christine about forgetting to water his morning glories.

"The joy of my life," Christine nodded in his direction. "Always teasing and always listening to tapes."

As I passed his tape deck on my way out I saw his collection—"Studies of the Beatitudes," "1 and 2 Peter," "Sermons from the Psalms," "Daniel and Revelation."

The secret of youth, I thought to myself. "They that wait upon the Lord, shall renew their strength. They shall mount up with wings as eagles. They shall run and not be weary. They shall walk and not faint" (Isaiah 40:31 KJV). I could almost see Uncle Alton with eagle's wings.

Personal Dividends

As a sophomore in high school, I never stopped to think where my words—and God's—might take someone else. But there they were in an old friend, standing right before my eyes at a get-acquainted time for new faculty wives like myself. My husband Mark was starting a new career as a seminary professor.

Peggy's presence at the retreat was no surprise. I knew her husband had joined the seminary faculty following several pastorates. But when I saw how God was using her to lead a committee of faculty wives that day, I was suddenly transported to long ago and far away.

Twenty-three years before and 850 miles away we had been tenth-graders together. There had been more differences than similarities between us then.

Peggy had lived near that small Pennsylvania town all her life. I was a transplant from the cotton fields of

Alabama. I had come to school with a blue plaid hand-me-down skirt. Peggy wore Pendleton wools. She swam in her backyard pool, rode her horse every Saturday, and had traveled in Europe. It hadn't been our similarities that drew us together.

Nor had it been any outward evidence of need. Peggy was surrounded by friends. She appeared to have all the personality, looks, money, and stability she could possibly desire. Nor had there been any great crisis in either of our lives to drive us together.

But there had been a slow, steady undercurrent of interest in each other's lives: I asked for tips on the game of tennis, which she played like a pro; I called to find out about her dad's back surgery; Peggy wanted to know about the little country church my father had pastored in Alabama and about the Christian club I went to every Tuesday after school.

We talked about things that were important to us— French, boys, teachers, parents, God. . . . A personal God was a new thought to Peggy. Her eyes wouldn't leave my face when I'd tell her how sure I was that God not only lived in heaven, but that He also lived in those of us who believed in Him on earth.

Peggy knew God had moved into my activities, my attitudes, and my dreams for the future. "He's not pushy," I explained. "It's up to you. Someday, when you're ready, God will meet you."

Now, twenty-three years later, I saw living proof that God's Word, both silent and spoken, never misses its mark. Faithfully invested in a ready heart, it will yield dividends!

Coming Home

Twenty-five years, and I'm coming home—down the joyous roads of my childhood. Today we take the narrow, two-lane highway that stretches south through endless acres of majestic Alabama white pine. I am lost in the beauty. The simplicity. The tranquility.

I'm coming home; leaving the confusing mass of eight lane traffic, the concrete and steel that futilely reach for the sky, and the people who are always in a hurry to be somewhere else. Alabama. Place of my dreams. Goal for my life. Where people have time to sit on their front porch swings and talk to each other for an afternoon or two. Where white frame houses stand strong and neat; where pecan trees shade the green yards; where white, fleecy cotton blankets the fields; and where the ever-present pine fragrance fills the air. Alabama. Where people work hard, never have a lot, but always enough. Where neighbor means everyone within a fifty-mile radius. Where someone always takes time to fix you a dinner of hot biscuits, black-eyed peas, and chicken in dumplings. Alabama. Why have I stayed away so long?

The road goes on, but we stop; dreams suddenly freeze into reality. The white frame house is yellow with age, and an old man in overalls is asleep on the steps. A ripped screen hangs loose from the corner of my bedroom window. No pecan trees shade the house anymore, and the front yard is a rusted-out relic of old bottles, cans, hay rake, and a car with all four tires and its insides missing. The porch swing is gone and half the porch with it. There are no fleecy fields of cotton beyond, only weeds. The lumber company has long since stripped the woods of its pine.

My neighbor who loved to fix me black-eyed peas and biscuits and always called me her "Black-eyed Ruth Ann," sits and stares at me with vacant eyes. I don't think she remembers.

"She doesn't even want to get out of bed anymore," her daughter tells me. Mary's kitchen is silent.

I close the door to Mary's house and sadly climb back into our Pontiac with its Illinois license plates.

"Why were the old days better than these?" the biblical writer asked. "It is not wise to ask such questions" (Ecc. 7:10). Mark starts the car and we head north in silence. I am thankful for my past, but in that brief backward glance, I also found contentment in my present. I am ready to move ahead.

Listen to the passing of time in your life.
What do you hear?

SURROUNDED BY
MYSTERY

SURROUNDED BY
MYSTERY

Living with
the Contradictions
of Faith

RUTH SENTER

CARMEL • NEW YORK 10512

The measure
of a mature mind
is the ability to hold
contradictory thoughts simultaneously.
—Thomas Carlyle

CONTENTS

SURROUNDED BY

♦ MYSTERY ♦

THE MYSTERY OF

◆ FREEDOM ◆

A JUST GOD

I watch the sun filter through the ancient oaks of Wisconsin's glaciated Kettle Moraine area. The early morning light slips silently from branch to branch. The couple in the neighboring tent watches the same sunrise through bleary eyes, accompanied by pulsing vibes from a ghetto blaster.

"They couldn't be more than sixteen," I say to Mark as we climb the hill for water. We both doubt the legitimacy of their night together in the Coleman tent. But the sun, that celestial goddess of all Wisconsin campers, shines just as brightly on their side of the ancient oaks as it does on ours. And hours later, when the moisture gathers into cumulonimbus and the heavens descend, we are pelted just as hard with the driving rain. Never mind that I'd just spent thirty minutes studying the book of Isaiah while the neighbors guzzled more beer and rocked to the Beatles. "God is fair," I say to myself as I walk away, "whether I understand his ways or not." For nature—that neutral agent of distribution—shows no partiality (see Matthew 5:45).

Neither does pain. Today I ride my bike down the street to the gold house on the corner of Thunderbird and Blackhawk. Death sits in this place. I feel it as soon as I step inside. Beth's wheelchair is folded by the door, and her cane hangs on the closet doorknob.

"She's too weak to even use them anymore," her mother volunteers. "We haven't walked in a week."

Tears gather in her blue eyes, and I try to swallow the tightness in my throat. I try to make it all go away, including this ugly nightmare of an inoperable brain tumor that sucks life from a fourteen-year-old, but I can't. I notice the family picture that hangs above the livingroom couch. It shows Beth nine months ago—a track star in full bloom. But now the petals are shriveling; the flowers are fading.

"Beth talks about heaven," her mother says. "And the neighbors are asking how this could happen to us because we go to church every Sunday."

"God is fair," I say to myself as I walk away, "whether I understand his ways or not." And pain—that neutral agent of distribution—falls on the just and the unjust.

I see the sun rise. I feel the rain fall. And I witness the impartiality of it all. No respecter of persons. Why should I expect anything different? Nature reflects the one who created it. God is just; he shows no partiality. Outside of grace, sin's penalty falls on all. "For the wages of sin is death" (Romans 6:23). Sin is sin. The consequences have been posted. God gives fair warning. No excuses. Rebellion, be it active or passive, calls for justice.

I understand God's justice because I remember rebellion—ten-year-old rebellion. My father dispensed the justice. "No swimming in the creek today." His ultimatum was simple, but I had plenty of excuses. "Jimmy went in." "I was so hot." "Everybody else's dads let them go." Excuses didn't matter; I had violated the standard. The penalty was swift and sure. Justice was done.

But then the father who administered justice reached for his big white handkerchief and wiped tears from his eyes. That day, justice and love were forever linked in my mind.

As I reflect on the paradox of love and justice, I remember where my lessons began.

My father's actions pointed me toward a heavenly Father who sits in the hall of justice, calls his creation to accountability, but weeps over waywardness even as he pronounces the sentence. " 'Oh, Jerusalem, Jerusalem . . . how often I have longed to gather your children together, as a hen gathers her chicks under her wings, but you were not willing' " (Luke 13:34).

Justice and love in the same person.

The sun rises on both sides of the camp. Rain falls on the tents of the godly and the ungodly. Sin contaminates all, but grace is available to all. I can be at peace about God's system of justice for I have confidence in the judge.

As a sinner who found grace, I know God, not as a judge, but as a loving father who continually calls me to accountability. One day he was my judge, but I also see him with a handkerchief as he weeps over my rebellion, issues my sentence, and then takes my penalty upon himself. I am acquitted. Justice has been done.

Somewhere in Wisconsin, the sun still shines on the tents of the ungodly, and down the street a fourteen-year-old withers away. "God is fair," I say to myself, "whether I understand his ways or not. For he is a God of justice."

FENCES

When we moved to our new home ten years ago, backyards stretched uninterrupted for the entire block. Kids ran the full length of the village green. No one worried about boundaries. Neighbors could cut across backyards without the hassle of fence-jumping and the guilt of trespassing.

Then came the age of the fence. I'm not sure who came up with the idea, but someone decided a picket fence would enhance the neighborhood. One by one the yards took shape. Full picket. Split picket. White picket. Split rail. Chain link. Batten board.

Not long after the fences sprang up, I noticed a strange backyard phenomenon. Up and down "the strip," neighbors gathered by their fences to talk. Some leaned into conversation, elbows resting. Others hugged the posts with a full-hand grip. Some rested their feet on lower rails. Others propped their backs against board and batten. Never before had news flowed so freely. Looking out my back door was like witnessing a scene from Robert Frost's "Mending Wall," " 'Good fences make good neighbors.' " The fences, confining though they were to our kids, provided a security that promoted adult conversation.

I have never read any behavioral science studies on the sociological implications of a fence, but I sense that they represent the human need for limits. I *have* observed what happens to conversations when they occur *over* something—a fence, table, or teacup. I have also heard about an oddly similar response in sheep. When fenced in, they roam freely over the pasture. Remove the fences and they huddle together in a frightened little clump.

Boundaries. Sometimes they make me feel secure. But sometimes they make me feel restricted. Fence me in and I immediately want freedom. It is my nature. When I had my tonsils removed at age six, I was a fairly peaceful patient until the nurse tried to tie my hands to the side of the operating table. Then I turned into a tiger.

A part of me still resists limits, whether they are diets, speed limits, or God's "Thou shalt nots." If the speed limit is twenty miles per hour, I'm inclined to take the straight stretch at at least thirty. Speed-limit signs and calorie charts remind me of boundaries. God's Word has the same effect.

Freedom is not untied hands, but understanding the value of restraints. I need God's boundaries, just as I need speed-limit signs, to show me the difference between obedience and disobedience. "Through the law," Paul says in Romans 3:20, "we become conscious of sin."

I have learned the need for personal boundaries to keep myself from overload. I know, for example, that one commitment per month outside of home and work is all I can comfortably handle. Defining my boundaries enables me to say no.

I cannot say I enjoy discipline. But I've learned that it provides the security I need to roam the pasture. For freedom, I am learning, is not an absence of limits but a healthy respect for restraint.

THE ROAD DOWN THE MOUNTAIN

P aths to the top of this mountain should be one way. No one ever wants to go down. This path leads to the sun—a place of peace and tranquility.

The glory of the Lord breathes in every lodgepole pine and giant fir up here. It stretches all the way to the glacier fields and pours itself over the rocks, tumbling downward in watery crescendo. It passes over the alpine flowers, and far below it reflects the aqua blue of the mountain lake. We have climbed so far I feel almost celestial.

Viewed from this pinnacle of majesty, life below takes on different meaning. Why do the heathen rage and the humans rush to and fro, frantically chasing their tails? What are those specks of dust that build castles in the sand and then watch them wash away with the first big rain?

Life in the clouds gives perspective. Authenticity. Simplicity. A log cabin provides our shelter, and a helicopter delivers our daily bread. We fill our cups from glacier runoff and breathe deeply of nature's pure air. No one wears a watch; there's no reason to look at one. We feed the ground creatures—the chipmunks and the marmots—and talk to the white-breasted grosbeak that sits on our table.

Surely this is hallowed ground. I can worship in this place. We write poems about majesty in our journals. We read about majesty. "O LORD, our Lord, how majestic is your name in all the earth! You have set your glory above the heavens" (Psalm 8:1). We sing about majesty. "O Lord my God, when I in awesome wonder, consider all the worlds thy hands have made . . ." We write about insignificance. "What is man that you are mindful of him?" (Psalm 8:4).

"Peter said to Jesus, 'Lord, it is good for us to be here. If you wish, I will put up shelters' " (Matthew 17:4). But Jesus pointed

Peter to the path down the mountain. As they went, Jesus instructed them about his suffering which was soon to come.

"God is a presence, not a place," I say to myself as I head down the mountain.

Once home I find a friend in the hospital, a neighbor who is dying, and a man who is drunk, depressed, and reaching out for help. "God is a presence, not a place," I repeat to myself. And so I look at the photographs of my moments on the mountain, remember what God did for me there, but reluctantly agree to live life on the plains.

SAFE WITHIN THE LIMITS

I am caught in conformity
   To this interstate
   To the flow of traffic around me.
I read the speed limit signs
But the miles per hour
Creep up on me
A little at a time.
I simply go with the flow
Of U-Hauls and gray Subarus.

Safe standard, I suppose,
Since they can read signs too.
So I clock myself by the crowd—
A conveyor belt of commuter traffic
Accustomed to traveling by its own speed limits.
"The law is broken only if you get caught."
We travel thus,
Until the blue light flashes,
And justice demands its due.

But
I have another way of setting a standard.
I push a small black button by my steering wheel
That sets the pace
Within the limits.

It relieves me of the competition—
   "That truck is passing me again."
The ambiguity—
   "Wonder how fast he is going."
The dread of the law—
   "Was that a squad car I saw?"

I sit back and enjoy the ride—
Safe within control.

Lord,
Your Word is my cruise control.
   It governs my speed
   Checks my excesses
   Restrains my impulses.
May I not forget to use it
So that I can sit back and enjoy the ride
Safe within your limits.

MEASURING-STICK SPIRITUALITY

How am I doing, Mom?" ten-year-old Nicky asks every third day or so. He's usually comparing the top of his head with the marks on the garage wall or with some landmark on his mother. What kid doesn't like to watch himself get taller? What ten-year-old doesn't measure himself next to his mother or red marks on the garage wall?

Personal yardsticks are signs of growing up, but not necessarily signs of growing mature. Growth can be an obsession—a measuring-stick mania.

"My husband is the spiritual standard in our house," I once heard a wife say. "Next to him, I feel like a shrimp."

What is this thing called spirituality, I began to wonder. Something we wear like a gold chain around the neck? Something we do like a household chore? Something we either have or don't have—like blond hair and blue eyes? Something we add or subtract and tally up on a scorecard?

"How do you recognize a spiritual person?" Mark asked a group of high schoolers one day.

Doug's answers never came quickly, but when they came we paid attention. "I don't think you know a spiritual person until they're gone." He didn't elaborate. He'd said enough, and I have spent years digesting his thought.

Philosopher George Santayana, in his book *The Birth of Reason and Other Essays*, states, "Health is not conscious of itself, but frees the mind for the perception of other things . . ."

Spiritual health is no exception. If I had to pinpoint spirituality in human form, I would say that it probably exists to the greatest measure in the one who is least aware of it. For spirituality, it seems to me, does not focus on *me* but on *God*. It asks not "How am *I* doing?" but "What will *you* have me do?"

Growth is not a plan we follow, a formula we calculate, a

manual we study. "Which of you by taking thought can add one cubit unto his stature?" (Matthew 6:27 KJV), Jesus asked during his Sermon on the Mount.

I do not see spiritual growth happen in my life any more than my ten-year-old sees himself add an inch or a pound.

Spiritual growth is not an act of the mind. I cannot think myself more spiritual any more than Nick can think himself two inches taller. He does not grow by watching growth charts but by eating his Cheerios and drinking his milk, by getting eight hours of sleep each night, and by playing soccer twice a week. Growth is a by-product of healthy living.

So it is with the spirit. Spiritual growth is the by-product of communion with God. Understanding this, I can put away my spiritual yardstick, for communion with God is a thing of the heart. Others may be aware of its absence in my life, but not necessarily conscious of its presence.

Spirituality does not draw attention to itself. Like air, it is necessary for life but invisible. You seldom think of it when it's present, but you know immediately when it's missing.

Others will see signs of growth, though. "My, how you've grown," Grandma usually says to Nick when she sees him every six months or so. The fact is, Nick has grown, and you can't help but notice the difference.

The same is true in the spiritual realm: The condition of one's heart is lived out in actions. Right actions naturally follow right thinking. But communion with God, not right actions, is the goal.

I look for an example, and I remember the one perfect embodiment of spirituality. Though not always recognized as he walked this earth, when he was gone, soldiers trembled and said, "Truly this was the Son of God" (Matthew 27:54 KJV). His walk with the Father was so close that he did not consider how he was doing on the spirituality polls. But when he was gone, people knew they had been in the presence of spiritual greatness.

JOY

Is it joy—
This ray of sunshine
That splashes itself over my front porch swing
    Where mounds of raspberry-colored pillows
    Are wrapped in summertime gold?
That reaches beyond to the crab apple
    Where the cardinal sings?

Does joy
Ride high above the amusement park
Where fun comes packaged
    In swirling cages,
    Pink cotton candy on a stick,
    And sailboat rides across the bay?

Or does joy
Leap from the pages of my ledger book
When all the bills are paid
And the green flows freely,
    Spit from some invisible reservoir
    Through a slot in the bank lobby wall?

Joy?
Perhaps it is my name
On the title page of a hardcover book
On credentials framed and hanging on an oak-paneled wall
Or printed on a four-color flyer
    Announcing the topic of my speech.

But does joy
Drip down the front porch swing
And run into little rivulets of mud
From the four-day rain,
    Turning raspberry-colored pillows to sog?

Joy?
An amusement park closed for the season,
Shuttered in motionless gray.
Like a great prehistoric monster,
The Screaming Eagle is encased in ice.
The thrill is gone.

Joy?
Bank account spent
While
Letters in white envelopes
   Demand payment for services rendered
   Or college tuition by the first of the month.

Joy?
When the only one who reads my name is the mailman
Who also brings letters addressed to 'Occupant'
Announcing this season's sale on garbage cans
And three-quarter-inch nails.

Nails rust; garbage cans leak.
And who knows
When the season's sales will start or end?

But as for joy
It is always and forever
A single thought:
Thank you, Lord, for
   Soggy pillows
   My name—known only to the mailman
   And the season's sale on three-quarter-inch nails.

For joy is
Thanksgiving
When there's nothing much to be thankful for.

THE TROUBLE WITH STRINGS
A PARABLE ABOUT FREEDOM

Like all kites, I have a basic need to fly. That's why hanging on a nail beside the furnace all winter made me so restless. "This isn't what I was made for," I'd say to the furnace as much as to anyone. "I need to fly. I have to fly. Kites were made for skies, not walls."

I endured those wall-hanging months by thinking of flying days to come. I pictured the wide open spaces of blue. I felt the powerful lift of the wind. I smelled freedom. "That'll be the life," I'd say to the furnace as much as to anyone. "No more basement blues for me. I'll find fulfillment in gliding to new heights. I'll show my power by soaring. I'll find freedom in drifting wherever I please. That's what real living is all about."

Spring finally arrived, and with it came billowing breezes and crisp blue skies that beckoned me to join them. I'm now doing what kites are meant to do—glide, soar, drift. If this is living, my spirits should be soaring.

But they're not.

I've decided it's the string. My problem is all wrapped up in this string.

I glide 500 feet above the yards, trees, and houses, but I can go no higher. The string holds me down. My spirit urges, "Go higher." But the string is always there.

I look down on the yards, trees, and houses, but they are always the same. The string holds me back. My spirit whispers, "Go farther." But the string is always there.

I look beyond the yards, trees, and houses, but I cannot reach the fields and meadows I see. The string holds me back. My spirit whispers, "Go alone." But the string is always there.

There was a time I needed the string. When I could hardly get off the ground, it got me up in the air and allowed me to fly. I needed all the help I could get, then. And the string was always there. There was a time when I didn't know direction or control. I needed the string then, too. And when the empty skies looked big and frightening, the string gave me security. There was a time when I didn't know how to land, but the string always guided me gently in. The string has kept me from lots of tragedies, I admit.

But I am experienced now. The skies no longer threaten me. I am confident. I know control and direction. Now I need fulfillment and freedom, not security.

There's so much I've not yet seen. So many places I've not visited. So many things I've not done. My world is so small. I've been so sheltered. The same cold basement walls. The same smelly furnace. The same old houses, yards, and trees. A kite needs to experience new places, new skies, new climates. A kite needs to fly higher and try new tricks. But the string is always there.

How much can a kite do with a string tied to it? How creative can a kite be when the person holding the string just stands on the ground gripping it tightly with both hands? How much of a kite am I if I allow the string-holder to keep tugging me right or left or pulling me in? How can I ever develop my own flying skills? How can I find fulfillment when I'm tied to a string?

"What I need is freedom," I said one day, as much to the furnace as to anyone. "I need to be my own kite, to do my own thing. Then I would really soar. Then I'd learn to feel, to experience, to grow. Strings are restricting," I added in disgust.

I would never be mature until I called my own shots. When I reached new heights, I would be wiser as to the ways of the atmosphere. When I got beyond my own house, yard, and trees, I would better understand other kites. When I made my own flight plan I'd be able to handle other decisions as well. "It would all be very educational for me as a kite," I said to the furnace as much as to anyone.

And then my big chance came. The call of the skies was louder. The pull of the wind was stronger. The smell of freedom was more enticing. But the string was there as usual, guiding me first to the left, then to the right, up over the trees, the house, and the yard. As usual, the string kept coming, a little at a time, just as I needed it. But I knew this was my chance to break free.

The big gust caught me as I was gliding about 500 feet up. I pulled with all my might. At last, freedom.

I don't remember anything after that.

Anyone know how to fix a broken kite?

THE MYSTERY OF
◆ SILENCE ◆

THE BRIDGE TO SILENCE

The world has been stripped of words. I park my car at the far end of the lane that bridges the river and walk to a quiet retreat center. River sounds and bird sounds greet me as I walk, but the only human welcome I receive is from a nun at the entrance. "God bless your day of quiet" is all she says as she hands me my room key. Her smile says the rest.

Silence follows me down the narrow hallways and turns the corner with me into room number eight, which faces the woods. The room has no TV or radio, no books in the desk drawers, no signs on the walls.

Here in this room with no noise, I wonder at the vacancy. I am not used to a world without words. The verbal barrage of the six o'clock morning news wakens me. Words partition my day and fill up the spaces in between. Instructions to my children. Information for my husband. Notations on my schedule. Messages over the phone. Slogans on billboards. Letters punched into my computer, spit out by a printer. Words exchanged over a piece of Frango mint pie. Ideas and opinions bartered like soybeans and silver on a commodities exchange.

But today, a day without words, I feel a certain loss. The silence rings in my ears like the ocean in a seashell. What does one do without words? I have come here to think, to study, to pray. Today I do not have to do anything on the run. I am not sure how to act.

I watch a thrush pick through the January snow in search of food. He doesn't come up with even as much as a berry. I wonder if he will survive until spring. Birds intrigue me. At home, bird books line my shelves, and bird pictures hang on my walls. I have three birdfeeders outside my kitchen window. But at home I never have time to wonder about birds. So today I sit and watch and wonder. The thrush is oblivious to time. And watching him today leaves me feeling nourished, not guilty for wasting precious moments.

The day ticks by with muted precision. I listen to my watch and read a devotional book. At lunch I try to decide what to do for the silent strangers who sit on either side of me as we eat our cottage cheese and fruit. I pass them the salt and pepper and feel a bit better. The rest of the time we listen to Vivaldi's *The Four Seasons*, watch the woods, and think. Someone pours hot coffee from my left and sets a bowl of rice pudding in front of me. I turn to say thanks, but the server is already gone.

Words are assumed, not spoken. We linger over the last drop of coffee. No one seems in a hurry to leave so I sit too. I can think of few times when I have sat with others and said nothing. I wouldn't want to be considered a wallflower. But today, it doesn't matter. As I walk back to my room I feel revived, even stimulated, not by conversation but by silent community. Perhaps I've sometimes missed community because of the noise.

Perhaps I've even missed the message because of the noise. When the carillon chimes afternoon vespers, I walk to the chapel, where silence writes its sermon on the velvet tapestry above the altar. "Thank you, O Lord, for your mysteries. For the wonder of myself and the wonder of your work." No choral anthem repeats the theme, and no one expounds on its meaning. So I sit and think about mystery while the afternoon sun creates shadows over the gilded letters.

I am surrounded by mystery. I do not understand sun rays, shadows, or gilded letters, but I praise the effect. I do not understand the ways of God, but I can praise him. I think of Beth, Jori's best friend from junior high who is being eaten alive by a brain tumor. Beth's life has no sun, no gilded letters, not even shadow. Sight, hearing, and speech are gone.

Thank you, O Lord, for your mysteries? To understand God I would have to unravel his mysteries, and to do so would reduce him to my finite level of understanding. So today I am at peace with mystery. I don't need to understand God to praise him.

No words have been spoken but I have heard much. Arsenius, the fifth-century Roman educator who exchanged his status and wealth for the solitude of the Egyptian desert, once said, "I have often repented of having spoken, but never of having remained silent."

I remember his words as I drive through evening toward home. The silence was not always comfortable, but I will not regret having been silent. For if I keep talking, I may end up with nothing to say.

LIQUID GOLD

Black giraffes
On iron legs
Drink of the crude earth,
Suck liquid life from its veins.
Mechanical haunches
Squat and strain
Dipping beneath
Crusty layers
Drawing energy—
Pipeline to Alaska.

I drive through Oklahoma
Down avenues of derricks
And I reflect on man's ingenious
Attempts to tap the Creator.
I stand on the shores
Of Lake Maracaibo—
Pool of Venezuelan wealth.
Offshore oil rigs rise like
Manhattan on water.
I reflect on my feeble attempts
To draw from my Creator.
"Wells of Salvation—"
Pipeline to the Spirit—
Wait for my rig
While the earth oozes
Liquid gold,
Mine for the drilling.
Amazing,
That I so often
Forget about my resources.

RAINY NIGHTS AND WOODEN CROSSES

We've come away from the cross. In our sleek, sophisticated society we allow no time for plain wooden planks that meet in the middle. I read *Architectural Digest* and *National Geographic* magazines, but I don't pay much attention to symbols that dominated the eve of Passover 2000 years ago. I feed my children, shop for groceries, put gas in my car, and drive to the post office, but I don't think much about the Roman style of execution and rocky hillsides shaped like skulls. Life is much too modern for archaic sentimentality.

But tonight calls to the past. My past. His past. Everyman's past. I slip into the semi-dark cathedral. One dim light from somewhere high in the vaulted ceiling makes me barely aware of muted figures passing by me as though in stocking feet. No one talks. Only the Gregorian chant from the far corner of the long, gothic nave breaks the silence. We never see the singers. They slip in and out by a side door.

All eyes focus on a simple crossbeam suspended high above the altar. The light from above shines directly on the cross. Otherwise, all is dark. There is no preacher. No Scripture text. No stained-glass windows.

"The Word was made flesh and lived among us for awhile . . ." The chant goes on, echoing off the vaulted ceiling. What does it mean to me—these simple wooden planks that meet in the middle?

I am in the middle of a fast-paced, upwardly mobile metropolis. But tonight I stop, study the cross, and kneel in shame for so quickly forgetting. This cross, like a wedding band, bonds me forever in love. I am loved. I am loved enough for Roman execution and a rocky, skull-shaped hill.

"Now let thy servant depart in peace . . ." The choir voice grows soft. The light dims. The muted forms around me start to move. I cast one last glance at the hanging wood and know I must return again and again. What tragedy to wander from the cross.

I pull my coat around me and head out into a rainy Seattle night. Returning to the cross compels me also to leave it, because the cross points me outward, to the world. I am loved, yes, but so are they. I see the lights of a million people in the city below. What tragedy should they miss the cross. I must return to the cross for their sakes, as well as for mine.

HOW SILENTLY?

Silent night . . .
> "But the crowds cried out,
> 'Crucify him. Crucify him.' "

Holy night . . .
> "Then they spat in his face and
> struck him with their fists.
> Others slapped him and said,
> 'Prophecy to us, Christ. Who
> hit you?' "

All is calm . . .
> "When Pilate saw . . . that
> an uproar was starting, he took
> water and washed his hands . . .
> 'I am innocent of this man's blood.'
> All the people answered,
> 'Let his blood be on
> us and on our children.' "

All is bright . . .
> "And darkness came over the
> whole land until the ninth hour,
> for the sun stopped shining.
> And the curtain of the temple
> was torn in two."

Round yon virgin, mother and child . . .
> "Who is my mother, and who
> are my brothers? . . . From now
> on . . . family divided against
> each other . . ."

Holy infant . . .
> "And carrying his own cross, he went out to the place of the skull."

So tender and mild . . .
> "And he cried with a loud voice, 'My God, my God. Why have you forsaken me?'"

Sleep . . .
> "Foxes have holes and birds of the air have nests, but the Son of man has no place to lay his head."

In heavenly peace . . .
> "Do you think I came to bring peace to the earth? I did not come to bring peace, but a sword."

Sleep in heavenly peace.
> "'It is finished.' With that, he bowed his head and gave up his spirit."

"And we beheld his glory, the glory of the one and only Son."

TOO MUCH OF A GOOD THING

It has not always been evil that has troubled me the most. Sometimes, it has been good things out of control. The wind becomes the hurricane. The river, the rage.

I stand today and look at such a river, a gentle creek gone wild. I have followed the creek through the seasons, felt the changes in its foliated banks: dormant branch, pregnant bud, full bloom. We have been one, the creek and I, in our stages, and I have found solace in my daily walks along its path.

But today I do not know this creek. Like an invading army, it ignores its boundaries, turns streets into swirling masses of sewer and mud, ravages homes, and holds inhabitants captive.

Motorboats take to the streets as though navigating the canals of Venice. They rescue residents—mostly mothers and children—from the four-feet-deep waters of this out-of-control creek.

Several days later, I walk by the creek again. This time it is contained, quiet, like a sleeping child, giving the illusion of goodness. But evidence of its excesses are everywhere. For as far as I can see, lush, green carpets have turned brittle, scrub-brush brown. Trees drip matted slush, and the air smells like dead fish.

I cross the bridge and walk to the street, where giant, yellow machines bulldoze water-sogged belongings into garbage dumpsters. Months, years, life-times of possessions trashed together in a mournful heap. I notice the mud-streaked face of a doll dangling limply over the top of a brown leather suitcase. I hold my breath as I pass this sewage reservoir of things. I say sadly to myself, "All because of a creek gone wild."

Who would guess that this peaceful meander of blue held so much potential for devastation? And who would guess that the good in our lives, when uncontrolled, can be our own worst enemy?

Why is this so? Perhaps because we build reinforcements only against obvious danger. We do not guard against the good. We sleep by the creek. It is harmless, gentle, peaceful, and restorative to the soul. We relax in good times, good friends, good things. But good things without restraint—good things in excess—may take a lifetime of cleanup.

Paul wrote to the young pastor Timothy, "Guard the *good* deposit that was entrusted to you" (2 Timothy 1:14, italics added).

If we had realized that good creeks could destroy us, perhaps we would not be suffering so today.

THANKS, LORD

My price tag was high.

You reached down deep
        Into your resources.
        It cost you blood.
            You gave me value.

You lifted my head
        And said,
        Walk tall and straight,
        You have nothing to feel guilty about.
            You freed me.

You said,
        See that mountain,
        You can climb it.
        See those rapids,
        You can cross them.
        You have nothing to be timid about.
            You inspired me.

You said,
        See your feet,
        They're made of clay.
        You're human;
        I'm God.
            You gave me perspective.

THE CHINA THAT STAYED IN BOXES

B rown masking tape crumbled like parchment under our fingers, and the yellow newspaper wrapping reminded us of fifteen-year-old news. Until that moment I never knew my mother had good china. But there it was in front of me, box after box of English Spode, white etched in delicate pink and trimmed in gold. Before the end of that sultry August afternoon in my grandpa's attic, we had unpacked twelve boxes of my mother's wedding treasures. I had spent fifteen years of my life eating black-eyed peas and turnip greens from plain fiesta plates—colorful but definitely everyday—while cardboard boxes stored the good dishes in an attic a thousand miles away.

"I put them aside for a while," my mother said as she unwrapped a covered soup tureen. "They didn't seem to fit down there." She nodded toward the south, her eyes misty. I knew how much she loved the poor cotton-farming families she'd left behind in the small communities of southern Alabama. She and Daddy had spent thirteen years of their lives in rural mission work.

Mother's packed dishes preached a sermon I've never forgotten. While reading Helmut Thielicke's *How to Believe Again,* I thought of her china. Says Thielicke, "When we find God, we are immediately taken into his service, placed on the track of our neighbor, and faced with an absolute demand."

There is no true service without giving up something. Sacrifice *is* an absolute demand. Some may have to set aside china or other signs of the good life. Others may have to empty themselves, as Christ did when he laid aside his rights to royalty (Philippians 2).

Mark Twain, in his novel *The Prince and the Pauper,* tells of the young son of King Henry VIII who changes positions with a poor boy in London. After Edward Tudor, the Prince of Wales, has donned the tattered rags of Tom Canty, he looks at the beggar boy from Offal Court and says, "And now that I am clothed as thou wert clothed, it seemeth I should be able more nearly to feel as thou didst when the brute soldier—hark ye, is not this a bruise upon your hand?"

With those words, the Prince of Wales, wearing beggar clothes, goes out to seek vengeance upon the soldier responsible for the bruise on his new friend's hand. Mistaking the prince for Tom, the soldier boxes his ears so hard that the young noble is sent sprawling to the street.

"Be off, thou crazy rubbish," he says as the jeering crowd closes around the poor little prince and hoots him out of town.

After years of anguish and grief as a poor beggar, the Prince of Wales is restored to his rightful throne, where he reigns mercifully.

Later, when "some gilded vassal of the crown, made argument against his leniency . . . the young king turned the mournful eloquence of his great compassionate eyes upon him and answered: 'What dost *thou* know of suffering and oppression? I and my people know, but not thou.'"

For the Son of God, sacrifice not only involved "laying aside" for the sake of another, but "taking on" the nature of a servant (Philippians 2:7). In an exchanged status, like that in Mark Twain's *The Prince and the Pauper*, lies the mystery of the Incarnation, the greatest act of putting aside and taking on. Christ exchanged royal vesture for humanity's tattered rags, a scepter for a manger, divine insignia for a criminal's cross. He gave up his right to power and reached instead for a towel. "Jesus knew that the Father had put all things under his power . . . so he . . . wrapped a towel around his waist . . . and began to wash his disciples' feet" (John 13:3–5).

I confess, I don't have my good china packed away in cardboard boxes in the attic. I haven't made great sacrificial exchanges or spectacular "putting asides" recently. I know the scramble for status. I have felt the appeal of name recognition and visibility.

But in the midst of a world consumed with what it can

acquire—status, china, salaries, or numbers on a church membership roll—I see twelve boxes of English Spode china packed away in Grandpa's attic. I remember the meaning of "putting aside" for the sake of another. I approach God and am confronted with a baby, a manger, a towel, and a cross.

THE DIFFERENCE

I could only see down.
      You made me look up;
      I began to notice the world outside myself.

I felt besieged.
      You melted my defenses;
      I became approachable.

I cried.
      You heard;
      I slept like a baby.

I felt pulled apart.
      You were my glue;
      I held together.

I was overwhelmed.
      You handed me one moment at a time;
      I relaxed.

THE MYSTERY OF

♦ LOVE ♦

LIFE WITHOUT MAGIC

Fairy tales were okay when I was a child. I was captivated by the idea that a plain-clothed kitchen maid could turn into a dazzling Cinderella and command the heart of Prince Charming, who combed the kingdom to find her, then carried her off to a land where they lived happily ever after.

During my formative years, when it came time for me to learn about virtues, fairy tales supplied them. Honor. Strength. (Have you ever read of a prince who *couldn't* slay the dragon?) Loyalty. Courage. The triumph of good. (The wicked witch always loses.) Fairy tales were a fun way to learn difficult truths.

When I grew up, I put my fairy-tale books on the shelf. But adulthood has created its own fantasies for me—especially when it comes to marriage. Madison Avenue hawks its wares: love sold over the counter in a bottle from Paris; happiness packaged with a weekend rate in Acapulco. Moonlight and roses. Candlelight and surf. Idyllic settings.

The prince is always handsome, immaculately groomed, smiling through perfect white teeth as he hoists the sails of his catamaran. Cheap fiction makes bigger-than-life men, always sensitive, warm, and attentive to the needs of the women in their lives. Who wouldn't enjoy such love? If I'm not careful, I fall for the pitch.

Romantic that I am, cold, hard facts don't set well with me. Marriage for me has been learning to adjust to reality. The white horse never came galloping out of the sunset. Instead, our Corvair broke down on the interstate just outside of Baltimore, and my young minister-husband and I spent part of our honeymoon in a garage. During the twenty-three years since our wedding day, Mark and I haven't galloped anywhere. Instead, we've gotten up in the morning and put one foot ahead of the other. My prince charming is fighting a losing battle with a receding hair line, and his noble quest for love is often lost in theology and three-point outlines. We often forget to light the candles before dinner.

Marriage has also been learning to live without magic. No fairy godmother has ever waved her wand over cluttered desks, forgotten grocery lists, or jogging clothes left on the shelf instead of put in the drawers. Magic words have never produced for Mark a wife who can sit down after dinner and watch the news with him instead of rushing off to clean up the kitchen. No kiss has ever transformed my hurried step into a slow and easy stroll. Living without magic is not easy, but I am stronger because I've learned to face reality. I know more about the grace of God in my marriage because I've lived without fantasy.

Marriage for me has also been learning to look for the good in the one I know best. Men at a distance always look better than the one I see shaving in front of the mirror every morning. Conversation with a male is always easier when we haven't had to unplug the stopped-up kitchen sink, balance the checkbook, or discipline a child. Familiarity blurs my ability to see good in my spouse. I may even stop looking for it because I am so busy looking for happiness.

In a poll conducted by *Psychology Today*, a man married for more than twenty years said, "Commitment means a willingness to be unhappy for a while." Such statements are not good PR for marriage. In fact, I wonder how many fairy tales would have sold had they ended simply "and they lived together ever after." Who doesn't want to be happy? Something would be wrong if I didn't desire a happy marriage.

But Jesus puts happiness in another context. "Blessed [happy] are the peacemakers," he said. Not happy are those who've never known troubles, but happy are those who have learned to bring peace out of the trouble—a foreign idea in fairy tales, where the nobility lives happily only after conflict has been forever banished.

Fairy tales are nice diversions in literature, but they promote an unrealistic view of love and happiness. God looked on his creation and pronounced it good, not easy or happy. And I suppose, despite my love for candlelight and roses and weekends in Acapulco, were you to ask about my marriage I would have to say, "It's been good." And according to God's standard, that's a high tribute.

A GIFT WRAPPED IN BROWN PAPER

There's a beautiful gift
    inside this package.
It's wrapped for
    protection;
    tied for security.
Stamped: "Fragile!
    Handle With Care!"

It's easy to loosen
    the strings,
to let just anyone
    tear away the
    wrapping,
to give the gift
    without commitment—
or hand it out as the prize
    for winning a game.

There's a gift wrapped
    inside this brown paper.
It's for keeps.
Non-returnable.
It's a surprise,
    a happy treat to be
    opened
    by the person
    to whom it's addressed,
    on the date marked
Forever.

CLOSE-UP DISTANCE

I had never seen Mark look more handsome than he did walking onto the platform in his three-piece, dark-gray suit and taking his seat behind the podium.

I know that man, I thought to myself as I watched him standing tall and straight behind the pulpit, leading the congregation in responsive reading. I did know him—the inside Mark.

I could tell by the pitch of his voice whether he felt nervous or calm, by the slope of his shoulders whether he felt discouraged or exhilarated, by what he did with his hands whether he was uptight or relaxed. These external clues of his internal feelings were unknown to all but me—the one who had lived with him for twenty-three years, getting to know what went on inside.

Suddenly the rows between us dissolved. I sensed Mark's closeness, his presence, our oneness, even though we were isolated from each other by pews of people.

The mystery of marriage, I thought to myself, *is that two people, though separated by distance, can be so close.* The sadness of it all is that two people may be sitting side by side and yet be miles apart.

I know. We were there once, absorbed in the busyness of life around us, caught up in the work of the kingdom, intent on ministering to the hurts and concerns of others.

We were busy doing, growing, learning—about Christian education programs for the church, about strategies for world evangelism, about Christian journalism and interpersonal communication. We taught courses at the graduate school, attended conferences, led seminars, preached sermons.

In the midst of our activity, we always found time to be together, jealously guarding our family hours. Somewhere over the clutter and clatter of life with the children, we would squeeze in a word or two for each other—details of parenting and daily transactions that kept the wheels of a household oiled and running smoothly.

When we dropped exhausted into bed at the end of the day, we would have little left for each other. But we'd say "good night," satisfied by tasks accomplished, people helped, experiences gained, progress made.

Our marriage could have survived that way for a long time. You couldn't say we weren't happily married: we were. We respected each other, were polite and helpful, remembered birthdays and anniversaries, and always called home when one of us was out of town.

On the rare nights we were home together, we'd build a fire in the fireplace after the children were tucked into bed. From behind the pages of a newspaper or a book by C. S. Lewis, Tolstoy, or Solzhenitsyn, we'd share our evenings together. We'd lose ourselves in a world of current events, science fiction, or human drama.

We could have spent a lifetime of evenings that way. In the security of the routine, the functional, the predictable, we probably could have maintained the status quo and played the marriage game indefinitely.

But we didn't. God in his graciousness disrupted our equilibrium. He sent along a counselor-friend and some written tests to show us how little we knew about each other.

We knew a lot about our world, our professions, our children, and about how to serve God's kingdom, but very little about each other's thoughts and feelings.

We had substituted the know-how of marriage for knowing each other. We had exchanged activity for intimacy. We had grown, but not together.

Reawakenings force us to assess our deficiencies. And somewhere in the assessment, we may discover painful truths about ourselves—our bent toward perfectionism and performance, toward activity and productivity, toward the immediate, the urgent. Hidden truths about ourselves keep us from knowing the truths about another.

But with painful reawakening comes joyful discovery—finding what's been missing but always within reach. Fortunately for Mark and me, the discoveries began.

We're learning, for example, to sit and talk to each other, not only at the end of an exhausting day but one morning a week of prime time. Sometimes we find our solitude while enjoying a hot drink at a little pastry shop, away from telephones and children. Sometimes we meet in our living room before dinner, just the two of us.

We try to talk, not about people we've known, places we've been, children we're rearing, but about ourselves and our relationship. We've learned that it's okay to talk about ourselves because doing so unravels for us a baffling and sometimes mind-boggling puzzle—the thoughts and feelings, words and actions of another person.

I cannot force Mark to play the guessing game. He'd run the risk of guessing wrong. So instead, I must offer a clear, direct statement, "I'm feeling lonely today; I wanted you to know."

We're also learning to ask questions rather than waiting for feelings to surface. When Mark says, "You seem restless today. What are you thinking?" I know that he has taken time to read my heart and wants to understand more.

When he says, "You really look tired. What can I do to lighten your load?" I know he wants to be a part of my solution.

We're learning to watch each other for clues. A deep sigh when he comes in the door and hangs his coat in the front hall closet tells me he's had a heavy day.

When Mark hears a high-pitched, high-speed chatter when we're in a crowd, he knows I'm feeling insecure. Looking over the crowd, he catches my attention and smiles or moves close to me and squeezes my hand. I know he understands. I am reassured.

We're learning that it's fun to spend an evening by ourselves doing nothing. A quiet strength comes from silent moments when we don't have to talk to anyone about anything.

When we do talk, we're learning it's okay to dream together about the future or reminisce about the past. These conversations become reminders of the grace of God in our marriage.

Are these moments wasted because I can't hold in my hand a finished product? Absolutely not. They are moments invested in oneness—a commodity money can't buy.

We're learning to establish rituals shared with no one but the two of us. That mystical union referred to in the wedding ceremony is enhanced by exclusiveness that stretches beyond the physical aspect of love.

During one stage of our marriage, hot peppermint tea and a doughnut on Wednesday nights at ten became a ritual. It was Mark's treat to me—served on a silver tray from our bedside table.

Praying together is becoming that kind of ritual for us. Our time of shared vulnerability before God. No one else hears. No one else knows. We lay aside our roles, our positions, our credentials.

Stripped bare of the trappings of life, we can approach God together as the people we are rather than as the people we'd like to be or the people others think we are.

Praying together is also an act of commitment; it shows Mark that his concerns are mine and vice versa. In a sense, sharing our concerns together with God establishes joint ownership. We are both strengthened and supported by the other's presence and participation in prayer.

Above all, we're discovering that intimacy breeds not dependency, but individual strength. Four days ago I kissed Mark good-by at TWA's Gate H3 and watched him leave on a service call for the body of Christ. The children and I drove home through rush-hour darkness, fixed ourselves a toast-and-scrambled-eggs dinner, and read books in bed until we fell asleep.

The other side of my bed was cold. All night I wondered where to put my feet. In the morning I smelled Mark's aftershave in the bathroom. His bottles were lined up neatly on his side of the medicine cabinet; his shirts were hanging limply in his side of the closet. All day I felt his presence, sensed the strength of his love, and waited for his call.

But life went on without Mark. The flu bug struck, a check bounced, a tire went flat on the way to church (along a busy two-lane highway with five children in the car), and a real-estate tax form didn't show up in time for our accountant. Monday morning the washer wouldn't start. Tuesday night a friend called to talk about her serious marriage problems.

Life's problems didn't wait for Mark to get back from his trip, so I did what needed to be done—at peace with myself and the world. For I knew that somewhere near Philadelphia was a man who would come home and say, "I love you, Honey. Tell me what I can do for you."

For the strength of intimacy, the joyful mystery of intimacy, is that when you lose your life to another person, you actually find it. Herein, it seems to me, is love at its highest.

RESTORATION

You can't smile at my sin,
It's not like you.
But still you smile at me.
You can't look me in the eyes
When I'm not looking at you,
> *But you'll wait around*
> *And our eyes will meet again—*
> *My heart will say, "I'm sorry."*
> *Your look will say, "I'm sorry too."*
> *I'll feel your arm around me*
> *And we'll walk on.*
> *You and I.*

MARATHONS AND PURPLE SOCKS

When the alarm sounded at 5:30 A.M., the last thing I wanted to do was face a day of city traffic, a crowd of 10,000, and sixteen-mile-an-hour winds and driving rain.

I had said I'd go along to watch Mark run America's Marathon Chicago. But that was before I'd known what the weather conditions would be. Surely Mark, sensitive person that he was, would understand how much better off I'd be at home.

I pushed the snooze button and settled back for another two hours of luxurious warmth. After all, I thought, I'd had a nonstop week, the children needed my time, and weekends were for refueling.

By the time I got to the end of my excuses, I was wide awake. Going into the city with Mark must have been a bigger commitment than I'd thought; why else would I be feeling so guilty about two more hours of sleep? My feet hit the floor. I knew I had to go.

So it was that I found myself under four layers of rainproof gear, frantically clutching my umbrella lest the stiff Chicago wind carry it away, watching from the sidelines as 10,000 runners took on twenty-six miles of streets. Mark's number was 6,942. From an umbrella behind me, rain dripped down my back, and my fingers, numb with cold, struggled to pour another cup of coffee from my thermos.

Four hours and who knows how many city blocks later, I pressed against the damp mass of humanity that crowded near the finish line. Knowing Mark would come into sight momentarily, I stood even with the giant clock above the finish line.

The rain had stopped, but the wetness had already caused the dye from my loafers to turn my gray socks purple. The banana bread and coffee I'd brought were long gone. But Mark was heading for the finish line. He had conquered.

As I wrapped a warm, dry blanket around him, offering my shoulder for him to lean on as we made our way to the car, I had a sudden sense of what support in marriage is all about.

"You know, today you gave me one of the most meaningful gifts you've ever given me," Mark said that evening as we sat in our warm family room and nursed his sore feet.

Until that moment I'd had no idea how much my support had meant to him. And then I remembered that love isn't love until it goes out of its way for another. With Christ and the Cross as my example, I'm amazed how quickly I forget the truth.

THE MYSTERY OF

◆ LETTING GO ◆

SOMETIMES IT RAINS ON OUR PARADE

H omecoming is supposed to be colored leaves, crisp sunshine, blue skies. Instead, we awoke to wet weather that promised to batter the area for twelve hours.

"Mother," Jori wailed as she bounded into the kitchen. "It's raining on our floats! And my first homecoming too."

The gloom did not lighten as we drove bravely toward the high school. Crisp fall was reduced to sog and saturation; the heavens came toward us in sheets.

But as we turned onto Prince Crossing Road, the dust flew. Just beyond the next hill sprawled a *dry* football field.

"See," Jori pronounced with glee, "the Lord knows where Wheaton Christian High is."

I felt a Bible verse coming—the one about the rain that falls on the righteous and the unrighteous. Somewhere in the world rain was falling on someone's float, even if homecoming was sponsored by Christians. Age fourteen was not too early for her to learn life's realities, I thought.

But the sermon would have to wait. Jori headed for the sidelines as soon as I pulled into the parking lot.

Later, as we dumped the remnants of homecoming on the kitchen table after a nearly perfect day, the phone rang.

"Mom. It's for you."

That night I didn't recite my Scripture verse to Jori. Instead I sat by her bed and eased her into the painful reality of the phone call.

The diagnosis on Beth, her good friend and Bible study partner, had been confirmed by a third neurosurgeon: inoperable brain tumor.

Jori disappeared under the pillows of her bed, unable to talk. When at last she found her spirit again, she said simply, "I knew it, Mom. I knew it was something awful."

As I kissed her good-night I realized I still had not recited the verse to her: "He . . . sends rain on the righteous and the unrighteous" (Matthew 5:45).

Jori was learning its message without her mother's sermon.

LETTING GO

Few places have I felt motherhood more painfully than at Midway Airport gate B3, a place of coming and going. I have waved good-by on the departure ramp and hugged hello on arrivals. But today is different. The sensation feels somewhat like having a tooth pulled—yanked from the roots that bury it deep. Today a part of me is being yanked away.

Eleven-year-old Nick looks impeccable in his new gray-and-blue spring jacket. A piece of his blond hair sticks straight up in back even though we tried to slick it down with hair spray. He hands the agent his ticket to Philadelphia as though he is buying candy at the corner store. He grins the grin of self-satisfaction.

"You're not scared, are you, Mom?" he asks, tucking his boarding pass into his jacket pocket just as I'd instructed him earlier.

"No Nick, I'm not scared. Just a little sentimental I guess. Mothers are that way, you know."

He grins as though he knows, but I know he cannot possibly know. He cannot sense that emotional umbilical cord that keeps me wanting to be his support system long after he's escaped the womb. How could he know how hard it is for a mother to begin releasing her child? He gives my arm a little squeeze just the same.

I hear the boarding call on the intercom and hold him tight for a brief moment. Then he is gone. He turns and waves before disappearing down the ramp. I watch window seven. As the Midway Metrolink turns east, I see the dim outline of a face, then a fisted hand with a thumb pointing upward. "All's in control, Mom," it says.

He's growing up—a frightening reality for a mother. I stand and watch as the silver bird shrinks to a dot in the blue. I can do nothing more for my son. The thought strikes an uneasy chord somewhere down deep and begins my pangs of severance. I knew they would come sooner or later, but I am not ready just yet. Metrolink Airliners don't wait around until mothers feel ready, though. They take off on schedule. I sense that is what is happening to my son.

I walk through corridors filled with a blur of people. I think of another mother who had to give up her son, not to a DC-9 bound for Philadelphia but to a reed basket on the river Nile; not for a week of spring vacation, but for eternity. My risk is nothing compared to the one faced by the mother of Moses, but I struggle just the same. Whether the destination is Philadelphia or Pharaoh's house, giving up is hard to do.

I turn the empty car toward home, comforted by the thought that sometimes it is in the unnatural act—the act of surrender—that we keep the most. The pangs of letting go will continue; there is no turning back. But down deep I know that both Nick and I will be stronger for it.

BIRDS HAVE TO FLY

I watch the storm move in from the southwest and listen to the tornado warnings on the radio. Dark cloud masses roll across the horizon. I go through the house closing the windows and thinking how glad I am everyone is home. Then I notice the robins, perched precariously on a middle branch of our backyard crab apple tree. Mother and two babies.

"She's not going to make them fly into this storm," I say to myself as I watch the drama unfold. The crab apple tree jerks as if it were tied to the wind by an invisible string. Mother and babies jerk with it. The babies flap their wings and almost lose balance. Their heads are still wet and wobbly—much too immature for these near-tornado winds.

But I am a mother of a different kind. I do not know what is right for robins. Still, I think it is a big mistake to teach your babies to fly when the winds are so turbulent. I wonder if she might not come to her senses and tuck them safely back into their nest where they belong. But when I come back, several hours later, both branch and nest are empty. The winds are still restless, but no baby robins lie smashed against the ground.

"Can you think of a better way to strengthen their wings?" Mark asks later when I tell him my fears for the robins.

I've never liked strong winds—not as a child when hurricane winds pounded the gulf coast near our home, nor today as an adult when tornadoes stalk the Midwest. Sometimes I struggle just as much with winds of a different kind. Often the mother in me wants to walk through my children's lives and close windows against the storms outside. I would not have them fly into turbulence.

But today, storm or not outside, it's time for me, like Mother Robin, to let my offspring fly. Jori has turned sixteen. I hand her the keys to the car and watch from the front porch as she drives away into the rain. Alone. We are no longer going with her. She toots the horn and waves good-by in exuberance.

I think also of another storm. When Jesus walked on the water toward his disciples, the Peter that climbed out of the boat to meet him was a child. The Peter that returned, though dripping wet, was a man who could proclaim with confidence, "Truly you are the Son of God" (Matthew 14:33). In the storms we often learn the most. I must trust my child to the storms.

The wind is still restless and the robin's nest still empty. The hands on the mantle clock crawl slowly through the evening. I pick up the newspaper to read, but mostly to wait for ten when Jori will return. We can never go back, Jori and I. When the time comes, robins must fly, storm or not. "What better way to strengthen their wings," Mark had said. I know he is right.

HORSE THIEF LAKE

We almost miss Horse Thief Lake as we drive on Highway 244 just west of Mt. Rushmore. Road construction takes us off the beaten path, the afternoon sun is low in the sky, and complaints are coming from the back seat. "We're hungry. Aren't we almost there?"

I'm not sure where "there" is. Just a clean campsite somewhere under the towering pines will do. As the road curves the children spot the lake and proclaim in unison, "There's a lake. Let's stop here."

I'm not at all taken with their idea. We need a campsite, not a lake. This place isn't even listed in our guide. Probably a crummy spot. Reason enough to keep moving. Besides, we have no time for swimming. My mind rehearses our evening routine. Set up tent. Pump air mattresses. Light the stove. Haul water. Cook dinner. Everyone has a job to do before we play.

But we turn down the dirt road and weave around the lake. Hidden in a far corner we find an empty space—towering pines, lake view, and all. I see the high granite walls at the north end of the lake. Tiny figures move at the top, then hurl themselves through the air. A faraway splash, shrieks of delight, and my worst fears are confirmed. This is not an ordinary mountain lake nestled high in the Black Hills. This is a "jump-from-the-high-rocks" type of mountain lake.

"Be careful on those rocks," I call after the children as they set out to explore the lake. They are back in a flash. "Please, can't we go swimming? We promise we'll do our jobs later. It looks so cool." I think of the long, hot hours in the van. Mark and I agree to the swim, and they are gone. I look toward the rocks. They only asked to swim. Surely, they won't jump off the rocks.

I volunteer for campsite duty while Daddy takes waterfront. Later, camp in order and dinner started, I head toward the lake to see about my swimmers. As I turn a bend in the path, I spot Nick poised on a ledge thirty feet in the air, ready to plunge into Horse Thief Lake. His daddy and sister are close behind.

I want to scream, to rush up those rocks and snatch my eleven-year-old to safety. He spies me on the path below and yells, "It's okay, Mom. Watch me jump."

Don't, Nick. But the words stay in my throat. I close my eyes in agony until I hear the splash.

"See me, Mom?" he yells after bobbing to the surface. He looks as though he has just conquered Mt. Everest.

Later, around the campfire, he talks with great pride of his exploits of the day. Next morning we break camp, head west, and I assume Horse Thief Lake is just another of life's inconsequential moments.

Several years later, when Nick was walking the peaks and valleys of junior-high years, he asked me one day, "Know when I felt real close to God, Mom? When I was up on those rocks, about to jump into Horse Thief Lake."

I give him a big hug. *Thank you, Lord, that I didn't say "Don't."*

The significance of that moment high above Horse Thief Lake sobers me. Any moment. Every moment. All are redeemable for God in the life of my children, if only I let go.

DEAR JORI

I stand by your bed and watch you sleep—innocent, peaceful, oblivious. A few blocks away another mother's child sleeps, in a different kind of peace. I know I must break the news. I stand outside your door and cry. Soon I will stand beside you and cry. Beth was your friend.

I wonder what I will say to you. Will we talk about the time in junior high when the two of you illustrated the entire book of James for your after-school Bible study? You drew rainbows over the bottom of the page about trials. Only the two of you knew what they meant. Maybe we will talk about your favorite song— the one you and Beth requested every Friday night on our local Christian radio station. "A Friend's a Friend Forever . . ." Maybe you will pull out the poem entitled "What Is a Friend?"—the one you wrote to Beth when you were in eighth grade. I look at the picture on your dresser of the Beth we knew before the brain tumor. The white porcelain frame with hearts around it was Beth's gift to you on your thirteenth birthday. Maybe we will talk about that birthday party. It would do you good, I think.

"She's in heaven now." I am startled by my own words. Your eyes open wide as though you've been waiting. "Beth" is all you say. I nod. You turn your face to the wall and cover your head with your pillow. "Mother, please, I need to be alone."

I close the door on your grief. The hurt burns in my throat—the hurt of your loss and the hurt of my helplessness. I want to take you on my lap and hold you close, the way I did when you were three and stubbed your toe. But you are almost sixteen now. You choose to grieve alone, at least for now. I listen to your muffled sobs. I take a new box of Kleenex to you. I sense I am still the intruder so I leave again.

Later I stand by you at the funeral home as you thumb through Beth's scrapbook. Together we look at her pictures and remember your happy times together—a concert, Great America, a slumber party. Your poem is there, printed in your neat handwriting and signed, "Your friend forever, Jori." I sit by you during the funeral. We hand each other Kleenex as we listen to the pastor read the poem you wrote to Beth. Someone sings, "A Friend's a Friend Forever," and I reach out and squeeze your hand.

I must be able to do something more. I am your mother. But today I cannot. As we follow the long gray hearse, I wonder if the greatest gift I can give you in your pain is the freedom to grieve in your own way, even when you choose to grieve alone.

WHERE HAS ALL THE LAUGHTER GONE?

Laughter doesn't live here anymore.
It went away with the phone call.
Tonight ours is a house of tears;
A broken heart
Unquieted love

I feel her ache
Like a soft pincushion full of pricks.
Why should reality have to start
When you're fourteen?
Only fourteen.
Too early to
Put away childish things.
I am forty,
But we cry together.
Hard cruel world
That metes out pain on the innocent young.
What does it mean to say "I love you"
And the next day change your mind?
I watch her as she packs up her heart
And prepares to give it back.
A black-and-orange football jersey.
She wore it everywhere,
Even to bed.
A stuffed kitty
(Her first significant gift)
That bore his name,
Only spelled backward
So it was not quite so obvious.
A happy moment caught between a gold picture frame.
The two of them leaning against a tree at summer camp.

Where has all my laughter gone?
Packed in a box with a shattered teenage love.
I grieve for her disappointment today;
I sorrow for all her disappointments tomorrow.
And the tears from her hurt
Etch themselves around my heart
Like icicles on a frozen day—
They don't go away.

I feel the lines of age;
The stripping away of my carefreeness.
Rachel weeping for her children.
By the rivers of Babylon we sat and wept
When we remembered Zion.
"Sing us the songs of Zion."

But my children's pain inspires no song.
Responsibility for them weighs on my spirit,
And the shower I get from a water balloon
Is no longer a joke.
Playfulness exchanged for a sermon
On how to be considerate of adults.
Whatever happened to fun?
Remember when water balloons were jubilation
And cartoons from the newspaper were celebrations?
Remember when jokes were funny?
Three cheers for life
And you and your children went down
With a last hurrah.

I walked among laughter once
And I remember:
A dad,
Three-piece suit and all,
Kneeling on the floor of Kay-Bee Toys

Zipping a race car
Bright red and yellow
Through plastic loop-de-loops.
Father and son
Caught together in
Loops of plastic play.
A time to laugh.
I hear their joy
Even as I walk on through the mall.

I remember laughter
In the middle of a Jewel parking lot.
Mother and daughter
In a contest of shopping carts.
"Beat you to the car!"
Milk cartons bouncing
Eggs rattling
But mother won the race.
A time to laugh.
And I feel the joy all the way home.

Lord, bring back the captives to Zion
Refill our mouths with laughter
Even when we must weep with our children.

SMILES, MILES, AND HAPPY MOMS

S mile, Mom! You look much better when you do."

Nick's words startle me. I haven't been told to smile since I was a kid in Sunday school and we sang, "If you have a little frown, turn it upside down. Everyone ought to keep smiling."

Obligingly, I flex my face, then close the front door and head toward Klein Creek for my daily two-mile hike. The late-afternoon sun is mellow, the park tranquil. But I cannot forget Nick's words. I cross the wooden bridge and wonder what prompted his admonition.

I consider myself a pleasant person. No dark shadows have followed me through life. Most of my childhood and adult years have been more like sunny picnics. I've known moments of pain—some private, some not so private. But on the whole, my life has brought more smiling than crying.

On the other hand, I have never been one to manufacture smiles just to make myself look better—or to make someone else feel better. If I've had a long day and my head aches, I don't rehearse smiles before my family comes to the dinner table. I think of myself as much too "authentic" for that. And I've always had trouble smiling into a camera. I avoid staged smiling whenever possible.

What, then, do I do with Nick's words? Disregard them as mere child's chatter or assume some serious deficiency in our relationship? What kind of a mother am I that my son has to beg for a smile? I decide that neither extreme is valid, but I will not ignore Nick's comment.

Long ago I came to the conclusion that it is wise to listen carefully to those who know me best. They give me the stripped-down version of who I really am. "Think about how you're coming across" is a line we use often with our children. I'd never thought to apply it to myself. *How am I coming across?* I wonder today as I pass the first clump of cottonwood along the creek.

Home is where you can be yourself—an oasis of authenticity. If I don't feel like smiling, why smile? The people who love me will keep on loving me whether I smile or not. It is part of the magic we call home and family and love—no conditions attached.

I turn west into the park. My favorite mallard sits in the middle of the lagoon, surrounded by sunset on water. I cannot miss the analogy of this peaceful scene. Why smile for my family? A genuine smile is a scene of peace. It reflects what is going on inside me even as the lagoon reflects the western sky.

What is in my heart eventually appears on my face. Jesus used different words to make the same point when he said, "The good man brings good things out of the good stored up in him" (Matthew 12:35).

I suspect that all too often the ones I love see deep lines of weariness, worry, and responsibility etched on my face—everything but peace. If a twelve-year-old could analyze his words, Nick would probably agree that he was asking not so much for a smile as for a happy mom.

A popular phrase says "Smile, God loves you." Although God's love is valid motivation for smiling, I believe God, like Nicky, is more concerned with my attitude than with my smiles. There will be days I don't smile even though I know God loves me. When I am without a smile, my family will have to take my word that I love them. But if anyone deserves my smiles, it is my family. If there is any place I should reflect happiness, it is at home.

I make the final loop toward home and cross Klein Creek for the second time. I am hot, my feet are tired, and a biker almost runs me off the path. As I drop onto our front porch swing, I catch a glimpse of myself in the window. Nick was right. I do look better when I smile.

THE BIKE THAT TALKED ABOUT GOD

Maybe God knew my bike was getting to be more important to me than God," Nick reflects as we sit on the front porch swing waiting for his ride to school. He is still struggling with the reality that his cherished bike, the one he built with his own hands, is gone—stolen from its usual spot in the garage. Two days after opening the garage door and finding it missing, he is still in shock.

"Why would anyone want to steal my bike? A whole year of building and saving . . ." He brightens momentarily and laughs over the many nights he slept with half a bike next to his bed. The day he rode the finished project down the driveway for the first time, we all stood and cheered.

Why do things and people we love sometimes disappear from our lives? It is a question as deep as the pain. I don't even try to answer it. I simply say, "Nick, your bike was stolen because someone wanted what you had. Today, God puts his arms around you and says, 'Okay, Nick, the bike is gone. Now, what can you and I learn through it?'"

Nick is quiet for a moment longer. Then he stands, hugs me, and is off to school. I know he is learning, not only about an evil world but also about a loving God.

THE SACRIFICE

No one said much at dinner. The empty chair said it all. The preacher cleared his throat and reached for his Bible. His eyes paused on the empty plate. His daughter never came.

The preacher smiled weakly at his wife. He wished he could say, "It will be all right." But he didn't know.

As usual, he read from the Bible. But his words sounded hollow. His mind took him far away. How far, he didn't know. His mind was with his daughter, wherever she was. His prayer faltered.

Where had he failed? His mind raced over the past fifteen years of his ministry. Life had not always been easy, but it had been good.

He and his wife, with her seemingly endless resources of quiet strength, were proud of their four boys and one girl. Their children were typical. Rambunctious. Fun. Intensely loyal to one another.

There had been storms at the preacher's house, but nothing that caused serious damage. He chalked them up to experience. But then the wind shifted. The preacher watched and prayed. When he saw the storm coming, he began battening down the hatches.

People across the hollows and the cotton fields of southern Alabama knew the preacher. For twelve years he had comforted them, steadied drunken feet, and pushed stranded travelers out of ditches. He had driven miles to take them to the nearest hospital in the middle of the night and had sat by the fire of one who earlier had pointed a gun at him. Yes, the preacher was always there.

People knew he would stop by to sit on their porch and talk. They knew he would hammer nails with them, bring them a load of firewood from his woods, come by with his car to take them to church. They knew he would marry them, bury them, and sit with them when they were sick.

They knew about the little churches he built. They gave him land and worked side by side with him. They came to hear him preach. They lined the crude wooden benches or sat on folding chairs under a tent. Many changed their life's direction as a result of his preaching. They grew strong. And when the time came for the preacher to reach out to the people thirty miles up the road, they cried and waved good-by but continued the love he had begun.

The preacher was a family man. When he helped deliver calves, he took his children. When he sat all night with a grieving family, one of his five sat with him. When he went to the jails, a small one went along. His children sat around fireplaces with him when he taught the Bible to neighbors. They sat on porches with him, hammered nails with him, made emergency hospital trips with him, gathered firewood with him, and heard him marry, bury, preach, and pray.

Now his children were growing up. Almost overnight, his daughter became a strange mixture of child and adult, calm and fury, delight and despair, laughter and tears, stubbornness and tenderness. The preacher loved her. He understood the passage to adulthood. He sensed her passage would be rockier than most, but he hoped to steer her around the boulders.

The preacher had based his values on Scripture. He hoped his children would do the same. But his daughter had friends with different values, and their values were beginning to overshadow his. Honesty, openness, truthfulness, respect, self-discipline, hard work, prayer, and obedience were becoming less important to his daughter.

The preacher hurt deeply.

At first came innocent spend-the-night parties with girlfriends. Then came scrawled notes sent home with her brother. "Dad, I'll be late getting home from school. I have to stay and help on a project. A friend will bring me home."

Then came flimsy excuses about why she didn't get home from her nine-to-five Saturday job at Elmore's Variety store until eleven and the hasty exits after Sunday dinner to go for a ride with older girlfriends. She never mentioned where their three-hour drives took them.

Porch lights stayed on and dinners got cold while the preacher and his wife waited and wondered.

They thought about their life of service to the Lord, of the three little churches they had helped build, and of the hundreds of people who needed them.

There had been tests, but they had passed. There had been discouragement, but comfort had come. There had been sacrifices, but they had not cost them their family.

They also thought of their daughter. Though they gained Escambia and Conecuh County, they could lose their own daughter. Would it be worth it?

They thought of their future. Every year, more and more people said, "Move up here. Start a church for us too." They saw their future in little communities without churches.

They also thought of their daughter's future. Could they expect to grow a healthy plant if they ignored nature's havoc on the tender sprout? As good farmers, they knew that a young plant having trouble needed a more suitable place to grow.

Their decision tore them from the people they loved. From their land and their home. From the ministry into which they had poured their life's blood. It left gaping holes. Who would shoulder the burdens? Who would love as they had loved?

But who could love their daughter as they could? Who could share her needs as they could? No sacrifice was too great. The transplant took place.

The East had churches with large youth groups, seminary-educated staffs, trained visitation groups, and Christian psychologists. No one needed the preacher, his firewood, his steady hand, or his car. Wood sold for thirty dollars a cord, retreat centers treated alcoholics, and emergency ambulance service came within three minutes to carry the sick to the hospital.

For a while, the preacher drove a bread truck and sold meat to feed his family. It was perhaps his greatest ministry. His young flower blossomed.

The preacher lost his church. But he saved his daughter. I know. The preacher was my father.

THE MYSTERY OF

◆ TIME ◆

LOOK TO THE ROCK

Most people can drive through Range, Alabama, and never know they've been there. But not if you are the preacher's daughter, coming home after twenty-five years. Highway 47 follows the old railroad line, then makes a 45-degree turn at Jackson's store. Just beyond the bend in the road is the white clapboard schoolhouse, once flour mill, now community center. The road curves through Miles Jackson's pasture, skirts Noah Bell's cotton field, and ends, for me, at the white cement block church with a tiny square porch on the front and two Sunday school rooms at the rear.

Tonight, twenty-five years have no meaning. I am fifteen again and the preacher's daughter. I slide onto the pine bench and take a red paperback songbook from the rack in front of me. Cardboard fans on wooden sticks still remind me of funeral homes and doctor's tongue depressors. We sing "There's a land that is fairer than day. And by faith we shall see it afar . . . In the sweet, bye and bye . . ."

I study the picture on the wall—the one of a little girl walking across a bridge at night with an angel hovering nearby. It hangs just above the gas heater, near where we huddled when the temperature dropped. The attendance board says 43 for last Sunday, and $35.60 for the offering.

I look at the faithful faces around me: Clevie, my bus driver, who still says "Yes ma'am" and "no sir" to everyone; Manse Edwards, who took us fishing in his boat and riding in his green pickup truck; Doris Bell, who made us buttermilk biscuits; Iverlee Jackson, who brought us our mail and delivered telephone messages because his store had the only phone for miles around; and Erma Ruth McCall, who my daddy led to Christ before the little church was even built.

Clara Pettus smiles at me from the third row and afterward gets tears in her eyes as she recalls the night my daddy sat all night with her family when her husband died. "It was 1955, April third," she says with the sound of sorrow. I notice how young she looks for 87.

Daddy walks to the pulpit as though he's never been away. His voice spans the years and pulls us back to the community we once were. I am suddenly aware that I have never left this place or these people. I have taken them with me. They are as much a part of me as my dark eyes and brown hair. I think of the prophet Isaiah who once reminded his people to "Look to the rock from which you were cut and to the quarry from which you were hewn" (Isaiah 51:1).

I must return to Jackson's store and the old flour mill to help me understand who I am today. I must stop at the little white concrete church at the bend in the road to remember my commitments to God. I am bound forever to Range, Alabama, and to Conecuh County Highway 47. Retracing my steps tells me how much.

MUSIC FROM THE GRAND CHICKERING

The Chickering grand piano looked as if it belonged on red velvet carpet in the drawing room of an antebellum mansion. Instead, it sat on gray concrete, squeezed between hand-hewn benches and a plain pine pulpit, in a little country church in Range, Alabama. Even against cement-block walls, the piano's rosewood casing and its intricately carved legs looked regal. As a nine-year-old, I fantasized about where the piano might have been. The governor's mansion in Montgomery? A plantation in Huntsville? The estate of a timber baron in Brewton? But its origins were not nearly as important as the role it played in a parent-child relationship.

The donor of the grand piano was a mystery. Someone had heard about Daddy's church and had written to ask if the preacher would like a piano. One day a truck arrived, backed up to the front entrance of the church, and unloaded the majestic Chickering. My mother, the church pianist, was especially pleased. The piano was a work of art, almost too fine to touch. I squatted and studied the delicate designs of the leg carvings; I looked at my image in the gleaming rosewood casing. I had never seen anything so fine. Daddy propped the lid open, and Mother said, "Well, Ruth Ann, aren't you going to play it?"

Me, play a piano that looked as if it belonged to court musicians? I was barely out of *John Thompson,* book three. But I took my place on the piano stool after Daddy adjusted it to fit my height. "The Spinning Song" sounded like an organ concerto. I closed my eyes and imagined a big cathedral in Europe.

Daddy assigned me the care of the piano. Every Saturday afternoon when my brothers and I cleaned the church, I went straight for the piano. I waxed and polished the mahogany until my brothers teased that I would surely wipe the casing away. On

Sunday mornings before church, I opened the heavy wooden lid. After church I put the lid down.

After school each day, I walked across the yard, music books in hand, opened the church door, and sat down at the Chickering to practice. From my place on the piano stool, I could look out the window, trace clouds in the sky, or watch birds flutter over the bean patch. There I enjoyed a quiet kind of solace—the gentle music, the clouds, the birds, the bean patch, the piano, and me.

One Sunday morning several years later, Daddy said, "Ruth Ann, how would you like to play the piano for Sunday school some morning? You choose the songs you'd like us to sing, practice them, and let me know when you're ready." At first I thought he was being his usual tease, but his face was serious. He really *did* want me for his accompanist.

I doubled my practice time. I started at the beginning and went page by page through every song in the red paperback *Gospel Songbook*. Mrs. Bushbee, my piano teacher at school, sent a note home that said, "Ruth Ann is making unusual progress in her music. Keep encouraging her."

One day I announced proudly to Daddy that I'd like us to sing "What a Friend We Have in Jesus" and "For God So Loved the World." The next Sunday when Daddy announced the songs, I took my place at the piano. My hands shook so badly I could hardly feel the keys, and I used the soft pedal for the entire song. I forgot a B-flat or two and played the wrong measure for an introduction, but Daddy thanked me politely when we finished singing, and after church Mother came to hug me and say how proud she was.

I wish I could say that I went on to become a concert pianist or an accomplished musician. Today I'm neither. But I did become our Sunday school pianist, and when Mother took time off to have another baby I filled in for her during worship services. I played the simple gospel hymns with little flourish but with great feeling and pride. It didn't matter that I would never be a famous pianist.

Mother and Daddy believed in me. They made me their Sunday school pianist even though an adult could probably have done it better.

Trusting your child is a theme as old as the story of Moses. In order to save her son's life, Moses's mother placed him in a waterproof basket among the reeds along the Nile River and left her daughter Miriam to watch over her baby brother. With a mother's statement of trust like that, it is little wonder that Miriam went on to become a great leader of her people. A parent's trust is a powerful motivator, whether it be watching over a basket in the Nile River or playing "For God So Loved the World" for Sunday school.

The antique Chickering piano no longer sits at the front of the little church in Range, Alabama. A smaller upright has taken its place. But in my mind I carry the image of that grand piano, and I remember what it felt like to have parents who trusted me enough to let me share their ministry. No wonder ministry is such a happy thought for me today.

WITH YOU ALWAYS

I am alone, wrapped in angry, atmospheric gray. The wide-bodied DC-10 vibrates with the wrath of the storm. For all emotional purposes, I am alone—just me and a planeful of meaningless others.

But I sense another. Moments earlier we had walked together to the end of the concourse. We have taken a lifetime of walks together.

The two of us walked together when the night gobbled up little girls and the path through the woods to a friend's house moved through mysterious shadows, when thunder shook the house and lightning pointed ugly spears in our direction, when hurricane gales whipped in from the coast, and when guns in the night shot bullets into the house down the road and drunks knocked on our door at two o'clock in the morning.

"Even though I walk through the valley of the shadow of death, I will fear no evil, for you are with me" (Psalm 23:4).

We had sat together at the airport gate, sometimes talking, sometimes not. But nothing was more important than sitting and waiting together. We have done a lifetime of sitting together. When the fish were biting at Manse Edward's lake, father and child sat in silence, bound together by a fishing boat and time. When a brown cocker spaniel died, father and child sat together and cried on an old log near the pecan tree that marked the grave.

"Even though I walk through the valley of the shadow of death, I will fear no evil, for you are with me" (Psalm 23:4).

When we parted at the boarding gate, moisture gathered in his eyes. "It's not an easy time," he said. "But life goes on . . . and God is with us."

With us. With me. With you always. In flesh and blood I saw the meaning. For another Father had walked with me through the shadows, grieved with me over loss, sat with me while I waited, flown with me through the storms.

I had seen God's love in the flesh of a father who was not just *for* me—but always *with* me.

THE GIFT THAT NEVER CHANGED

I t is a simple, red, leather-bound Bible. But to me it is much more than words in leather wrapping. Today it links my past and present. It has been a part of every transition. Today, it calls me to remember . . .

An early morning sunrise. I am eight years old. Seldom do I get up this early, but today I am on my way to camp. Anticipation keeps me from sleep. My suitcase, packed and ready, sits waiting at the end of my bed. I tiptoe through the pre-dawn house. I wonder, *will everything be the same when I get back? Will my dog Susie still know me? Will mother still remind me to put my sweater on and please not to crack my gum so loudly?*

I find mother on the front porch swing with her red leather Bible open in her lap. I sit beside her, and she talks to God about camp and about me. I am less afraid.

A rainy night in August. I am eighteen years old. The same blue suitcase sits packed and waiting at the end of my bed. This time a trunk and an assortment of boxes and bags are stacked nearby. I look around the little room—the one corner of the world I'd called my own. *Will it still be mine after a semester of college? Will mother still come and sit on the edge of my bed and talk after I come home from an evening out? Will my brothers still borrow my radio and eavesdrop on my phone conversations? Will my Manheim Central High School pennants still be hanging on the wall?*

I go toward my parents' room to say one last good night. Mother is kneeling by her bed, her red leather Bible open before her. I kneel beside her as she talks to God about college and about me. I am reassured.

A house full of wedding guests. I am twenty-one years old. Cars with out-of-town license plates line the circular driveway that leads to the front porch. I wait for the clock to run its cycle. This time tomorrow night, I will be Mark's wife. The thought has a certain mystery about it—like trying to imagine what life on the moon would be like. I do not know whether to laugh or cry.

I walk through the silent space that has been my home. The long wide hallway houses the family photo gallery. I look at myself as a nine-month-old and wonder what my own daughter will look like someday. I wonder what will change now that I am leaving home for good. *Will Daddy still give me bear hugs and call me his little girl? Will Mother still ask if I need a sweater? Will she still bake my favorite treat—Moravian Sugar Cake—when I come home?*

I walk past the living room. Mother is sitting in her favorite chair, her red leather Bible open in front of her. I sit beside her. With wedding gifts piled high all around us, Mother, as though giving me one last gift, talks to God about my marriage and about me. I am ready for the unknown.

I don't see many red leather Bibles anymore, and I don't kneel much to pray. Most of my prayers are on the run, not on my knees. But today I pick up Mother's red leather Bible and wonder what more valuable gift I could leave my children than lasting memories of a mother who read her Bible and prayed for her children.

WHEN THE MOON DOESN'T SHINE

U sually the moon shines bright on clear May nights in eastern Pennsylvania. But tonight the moon is missing. All is dark. I notice brown circles under the lamp in the hall when mother welcomes our 2:00 A.M. arrival from Illinois. I also notice brown circles under her eyes. Spots I'd never noticed before. Tired skin under gentle folds.

But here she stands, my mother for forty years. I sense an accumulation of nights waiting up for home-coming children, as though the years have cast shadows from the lamp onto her face. I see the years in the black and blue veins that have just this week felt the heart specialist's probe. I hear the years—like the ocean ringing in a seashell—in the doctor's diagnosis. "Red flag . . . enlarged heart . . . slow the pace . . ." I stare into uncertainty. Mother has been a steady pulse through the years. Tomorrow has been an assumed promise—a grand procession of family weddings, births, graduations, music recitals, ordinations, Christmas, Easter, Thanksgiving. Time has been an event, not a sequence.

As I look at Mother, I sense that someone has wound the clock. Time now has a cadence. Years have become increments. History has a beginning and an end. I shiver in the early morning chill. But then Mother's arms wrap me in warmth, and I am home. A forty-year-old child reassured by her mother's touch. There is no time in touch. Welcoming arms know not the years.

I hear the tea kettle whistling. Freshly baked chocolate chip cookies wait on the old ironstone plate that once served cookies from Grandma Hollinger's kitchen. Mother's chocolate chip cookies and Grandma Hollinger's ironstone plate pull me back into timelessness. We sip peppermint tea and laugh over a silly story Daddy tells. Our laughter drowns out the clock. There is no time in laughter. Mother laughs the hardest of all. Dark circles. Tired circles of joy. Her children are home.

For a moment I forget bruised veins and ticking clocks. I am held together by things that do not change—a mother's early morning welcome, freshly baked chocolate chip cookies, an ironstone plate, peppermint tea, a mantel clock, and laughter. I am held together by a God who does not change. I know the God of time who is yet above time. I see tonight in my mother's face the strange paradox of time and timelessness. A rare glimpse of the divine.

MAYBE NEXT YEAR

You're not coming home for Christmas?" Mother's gentle voice on the other end of the line conveys a trace of hurt. She struggles to recover.

"It just won't be the same," she says. "I know eight hundred miles is a terribly long drive, especially with the cost of gas these days. And we did just see you in September. But it will be different, not having you here to celebrate."

Her voice regains its strength.

"Well, we can send the presents United Parcel and call you Christmas day," she says. "And this way the children won't have to miss their Sunday school program."

I am relieved that she sees it my way. Mark and I are sure we have made the right decision.

Now that Nick and Jori are getting older, spending the holidays with their friends has become more important. They don't enjoy being cramped up in the back seat of a car for fifteen hours one way while their friends toboggan in freedom down snowy slopes.

"Nobody else goes to his grandma's house *every* Christmas. We miss out on all the fun around here."

"There's nothing to do there except play Parcheesi and talk about the old days. Can't we stay home? Just this once?"

They are right. It is time we start our own Christmas traditions. Who says every Christmas celebration has to have a twenty-four-pound turkey and sixteen people around the dining table?

What about a dinner for four in the peace and tranquility of our own home? I will prepare my own recipes and serve food on Christmas dishes I've never had a chance to use.

We will enjoy opening presents, just the four of us, on Christmas morning. For once we won't have to rush through the evening gift exchange on December 20 to get ready to leave the next day on that long drive to Grandpa's house.

I won't have to sit Indian style in the car, my legs tucked underneath me to avoid a foot encounter with the thermos, picnic basket, books, and game bag.

We won't have to feed dollar bills to greedy toll booths, tolerate salt trucks that spit chemicals all over our windshield, or endure grumpy children who argue and complain in the back seat.

"When are we gonna get there? Daddy, he's on *my* side. Yes, he is! His foot is over the hump."

"There's nothing to do. I already read all my books. You mean we have seven more hours to go?"

"My tummy hurts. I think I'm gonna throw up."

Tonight I am far from childish chatter, hungry toll booths, and a cramped front seat. Jori has just lit the last candle on our Advent wreath. And Nicky, garbed in bathrobe and towel, is reading a story about the little shepherd boy.

A smooth order eases us through the evening. I'm glad we are home, just the four of us together on Christmas Eve. I have nothing to do but sit back, relax, and reflect upon the mystery of the God-Child.

But the evening has a strange ambivalence. The oak log spits its red-hot embers against the fireplace screen, and something sad burns in the sparks. The glowing log ejects a part of its core, the fiber that made it oak.

What about my family, my extended family? Having Christmas for four certainly doesn't mean we have permanently rejected grandparents, aunts, uncles, cousins.

I try to convince myself, but I feel disconnected from my old home, as if I've forgotten a part of Christmas.

For the third time, I turn the stack of Christmas records and sweep together the scattered popcorn kernels.

The children spread their sleeping bags in front of the blazing hearth—a new family tradition Jori has suggested.

Grandma's house has no fireplace. The children hang their

stockings along the staircase banister. After all the little cousins are tucked safely in bed, Grandpa fills the stockings.

I move my rocker closer to the roaring fire and watch as the once solid log crumbles into ashes. From somewhere in the night, I hear muffled sounds of carolers coming closer.

"We wish you a merry Christmas, we wish you a merry Christmas . . ."

Peering from the front windows, we see a group of neighbors lined along our driveway. Their carols draw me back to past Christmases.

Caroling on Christmas Eve was our family tradition. We'd sing and then give out baskets of Mother's sandtarts and holiday spritz to some of the older folks in the neighborhood. They always looked forward to our visits. Some told Mom and Dad that they almost cried when they saw us coming.

"You don't see many families like yours anymore—having fun and doing things together. Everybody's too busy. Keep bringing those children by to see us, even if there are sixteen of you. We love to see 'em all."

So Daddy promised he would.

I knew he felt proud to have all of us there, singing together, throwing snowballs at each other, racing down the streets, and sliding on the firmly packed snow—just as we'd done when we were kids.

By the time we had delivered the last basket, our voices would be cracking with cold on the high notes of "Joy to the World." We'd trudge back up the hill to the sprawling old house. White electric candles shone from the windows, and brown-bag luminaries lined the circular drive.

Uncle Ed supervised the brown-bag operation. He directed big and little hands in filling the paper bags half full of sand and in carefully anchoring the candles.

At twilight we all gathered at the top of the driveway and held our breath as Grandpa created magic by going from bag to bag lighting the candles.

No one said a word. We cherished the moment.

"Sons [and daughters] are a heritage from the LORD, children a reward from him. Like arrows in the hands of a warrior are sons born in one's youth. Blessed is the man whose quiver is full of them" (Psalm 127:3–5).

That was Grandpa's favorite verse. He quoted it Christmas Eve as we all gathered around Grandma's ninety-five-year-old table that had belonged to her grandmother.

It took all six table leaves, two of the longest tablecloths Grandma could buy, and every chair in the house, but we all fit— all sixteen of us.

From Alabama, Illinois, New York, and just the other side of the hill—we all came to be together, to hear our father read, and to watch our mother light the candles in the center of our Christmas Eve communion table.

From his well-worn Bible, Dad would read: "This do in remembrance of me . . ."

"Because God loves you and I love you, I give you this bread, this drink." Dad said it to the person on his left, and the message continued around the table.

Five or sixty-five—age didn't matter at this setting. We were drawn together by the common blood running through our veins and by that which ran from the cross.

Grandpa prayed. Some of us wiped away tears. Others held hands under the table. The men cleared their throats.

As we ate our traditional cream of potato soup, homemade rye bread, and Grandma's special Christmas salad that looked like a glowing candle, we knew we had experienced true kinship.

But most of all, we celebrated—as the men and boys fixed Christmas breakfast, as Uncle Daryl played Bach and Beethoven on the old player piano, as Denny read excerpts from his seminary dissertation.

The afternoon of Christmas day ushered in amateur hour. Nine-year-old Jori, adorned in a long dress and a shawl from Grandma's attic, made her organ debut with "Jingle Bells" and "Deck the Halls."

Three-year-old Jonathan introduced his new Ernie and Bert puppets, one on each hand, and gave us his rendition of "Sesame Street."

Uncle Mark set up the projector and transported us to old grist mills and clear mountain streams.

Uncle Ed played folk tunes on the mountain dulcimer he had made, and Grandpa read from his ageless book of verse and poetry. He remembered my favorites, the ones I begged him to read when I was only six and still sitting on his lap. Grandma donned an old-fashioned pilgrim's dress. Holding the children spellbound with her gentle voice, she read "The Courtship of Miles Standish."

I read my most recent story, one about visiting a crippled children's hospital, and Aunt Mary Ann served us her Flan Küchen, a fruit pastry she'd learned to make during her student year in Germany. Then we all leaned back and breathed deeply.

In the quietness, we could count the ticks on the mantel clock. Suddenly we were all children again. One by one, we had offered our gifts to each other. They were not wrapped in silver paper and red bows, but in the diverse talents and personalities that combine to make our family a reservoir of entertainment and fascination.

Another Christmas celebration had come and gone. From it we had drawn a storehouse of memories that would carry us until next year.

We found security in knowing that next year the old white house on the hill with its red sign on the door would welcome us, that the mantel clock would still be ticking, that Grandpa would light the luminaries, serve communion, and secretly tuck goodies into children's stockings.

Another oak log crumbles through the fireplace grate as our fire burns low.

I stand and shake myself from my reveries. Then I glance at the children, wrapped in their sleeping bags, sound asleep, and Mark, dozing on the couch.

No. We can't live in the past. Things change. Children grow up. New family units emerge. Time for new traditions.

But what about the traditions that still live? Why bury them before they're dead?

I hear Grandma's old mantel clock. I smell her bread and taste her thick, savory cream of potato soup.

But that was then. This is now. What about my home, my family, our traditions?

I move listlessly through the last moments of the evening. I fill the stockings with miniature treasures, check the turkey, put another log on the fire, and join my sleeping family.

Families were meant to be together, I think as I wait for sleep. Suddenly I understand my Christmas Eve feelings of loss.

Even more important than memories of brown-bag luminaries, caroling, snowball fights, and the Hollinger amateur hour are the people of those memories. Our people. Our family extended.

I close my eyes and see their faces. Little do I know that next Christmas one face will be missing—that we will live with only memories of when we were a family of sixteen.

In years to come, it will always be our people—Grandma, Grandpa, aunts, uncles, cousins—that will call us home again.

Next year, next year for sure, we'll go home for Christmas.

THE MYSTERY OF

◆ FRIENDS ◆

THE ALABAMA CONNECTION

We have little in common. My skin is white; theirs dark. I live in a white, five-room frame house down the blacktopped road. They live in a row of red-tile hovels, each with two rooms, a front and back door, cement floor, and a small fireplace for heating in winter. My house has indoor plumbing; their only source of water is the creek that runs past the far end of Mr. Huxley's turpentine still. I wear hand-smocked cotton frocks. They wear hand-me-downs made from flour sacks; size and shape don't matter. Sometimes Mr. Huxley brings yard goods from town and sells them at the commissary. Then mothers sew, and the clothes are passed through the community for generations to come. My daddy builds churches and preaches sermons. Their daddies work in the woods all day, tapping the pines for the resinous sap.

But here we are, a union of opposites, walking together down the dusty Alabama truck trail that cuts through the middle of the turpentine still. We are partaking of place, their place, a school where they write on a long, wobbly table and sit for six hours on backless benches. They are proud to have a visitor sit with them on their benches. They don't mind that their school is also their church on Sunday or that the outside looks exactly like the red tile of their homes.

Later we push into the inner sanctum of their community, past the dense undergrowth that lines the creek. Here mothers wash clothes and children take Saturday afternoon baths. We hunt for tadpoles and carry them home in tin cans.

We stop by the commissary. Someone buys an Eskimo Pie, breaks it into fourths, and hands me the largest piece. Though I'm an outsider, I share with them the elements of life.

White folks didn't visit turpentine stills in those days. Black folks didn't take you in. But that day they did. They'd never seen me before; they knew only that my daddy had buried Aunt Kora's son. Aunt Kora was white, but she lived next door and bought her supplies at the commissary. Black and white folk alike all loved Aunt Kora.

Today, years later, the red-tile hovels still stand, but the people are gone. I drive by to see what the years have done, and I remember that "I was a stranger and [they] invited me in" (Matthew 25:35). What higher praise could be given any person, any community?

WHAT MR. MANSEY TAUGHT
(BESIDES BIOLOGY)

Some things about high-school biology class I'd rather not remember. I have vague impressions of frogs and formaldehyde, platelets and amoebas, and other sights and smells I've tried to forget. But over the years since Bio 101, I've realized that I learned something I'm glad I didn't forget. It had nothing to do with science, though. It had to do with friendship.

Emily and I shared a lab table, but our friendship didn't begin with disected frogs and microscopes. I thought I knew her pretty well. She was a transparent kind of friend. I could tell, for example, how she and her mom were getting along by the way she answered the phone. And her driving style after school told me how her biology exam had gone eighth period.

Biology was Emily's barometer. A test score of 98 or above sent her soaring. Ninety-seven or below plunged her into despair. Emily never left any doubt about how she felt. I admired her for her honesty, so I put up with her mood swings.

My approach worked for a while. I'd either ignore Emily's lows or try to talk her into getting more sleep the next night. If I waited, her mood leveled out. Our friendship didn't require explanations or analysis. I left those kinds of exercises to the adult population. Friendship was for fun, not for psychoanalysis. I had never talked about my own feelings or been particularly concerned that others know what they were, so I didn't think it was important to explore someone else's.

Sometimes, however, I could not dismiss Emily's feelings so easily. One day I walked into the biology lab and found her sitting by the trash can vigorously ripping pages out of her blue biology notebook and, with equal vigor, depositing them in the large circular file beside the door. I knew those pages represented hours of careful, agonizing research for an assignment due in three weeks.

"This project is a total dud," Emily sputtered between the rips. "And to think I really believed I could be a biologist someday." She didn't bother to look at me when she said it.

It took a minute before it hit me that she was dumping half a quarter's worth of research. I tried a last-minute salvage job.

"Emily, listen to me, you've worked for weeks on that research. That's great stuff. I've read some of it. You are terrific in this class. If you had biology grades like mine you'd have reason for despair."

My words had little effect. The ripping continued. As I stood by helplessly and watched, Emily resolutely destroyed her biology project.

"Come on, Ruth. You know this is no good. Sloppy work. No conclusions. Even my experiment flopped. Some scientist."

By this time her behavior had started to irritate me. It made no sense. She knew she was good at biology. I knew she was good at biology. Everyone in the class knew she was good at biology. In fact, she was Mr. Mansey's only hope for the future from the entire sophomore class. She had come close to winning a science scholarship that usually went only to seniors. I took it as my moral obligation, in the name of friendship, to set her facts straight.

"Emily, you're at the top in biology. You know that. What's the deal? Mr. Mansey never said your project had to be perfect, though yours probably is. Here, let me help you get it out of the trash."

That was one step too far. "Just let me alone, Ruth!" She had never said that to me before. I was stunned. What should I do? Keep on coaxing her? Leave? Stand around and wait for her mood to shift? Step between her and the trash can and dig her report out as fast as she tossed it in?

As I stood there in indecision, Mr. Mansey returned from a faculty meeting. I saw him at the door and rushed over.

"Mr. Mansey. Emily just dumped her project," I blurted out like a three-year-old tattling on her friend. "She says it's not good enough. I think it's terrific."

I waited for Mr. Mansey to pick up my theme. Instead he pulled up a lab stool, sat down, and pushed his glasses up on his nose—the way he always did when deep in thought. For a long time he did not speak.

I felt a critical need for words right then, not silence. Mr. Mansey apparently felt otherwise, but at last he cleared his throat.

"Emily, not getting that scholarship was a big disappointment to you, wasn't it? I guess I wasn't aware that it meant so much to you. You're feeling that the committee was unfair, aren't you?"

His words were magic. Emily spun around on her lab stool, laid her empty blue notebook on the table, lifted her head high, and looked straight into Mr. Mansey's face.

"Yes," she said spiritedly, "that committee was terribly unfair. They penalized me for being a sophomore."

I listened in amazement as Emily's pent-up hurt came pouring out, this time in words, not actions. I'd had no idea she felt so deeply about losing the scholarship. I only knew she had been sort of mopey the last day or two. I never thought to connect the two, even though she had told me all about the scholarship, her application, the committee interview, and finally about the rejection. I hadn't thought about what it would feel like to lose something you really had your heart set on.

Years have passed since sophomore biology, but I've thought frequently about Mr. Mansey. He may not have taught me much about biology, but he taught me a lesson about friendship I'll never forget. I learned that facts, no matter how true, are not always the best help for frustration, discouragement, or hurt feelings. Sometimes all people need is the assurance that we know and care about how they feel.

'TIS BETTER TO HAVE LOVED AND LOST

J oan was all I ever wanted in a friend—fun, pretty, loving, fresh, creative, intelligent. We found each other in the crowded confusion of registration line on the first day of camp. Something about her made her stand out from the other 200 new faces around me—some mysterious chemistry between us made me feel as if she were a friend from long ago and we were just picking up where we had left off.

During the week an invisible magnet pulled Joan and me together. We went out of our way for each other. She dropped by my cabin on her way to the swimming pool, even though the pool was in the opposite direction. When I ended up at the back of the lunch line, she forfeited her up-front spot so she could stand and talk with me. I gave up horseback riding to go canoeing with her.

Whether sitting around a campfire, watching movies in the pavilion, or listening to a speaker in chapel, I always reserved the seat next to me for Joan. She produced a warm, secure, happy feeling in me. I felt safe with her. I could bring her into my room without having to clean up the mess. She didn't probe areas I was not yet willing to open for public inspection. I trusted her, even with my closed doors and closets.

Joan and I never had to work at conversation. We talked about the past and our dreams for the future. But we talked mostly about the present—boys and dates, which kind of pop we liked best and why, how stupid we thought the summer fashions were, whether dew rises or falls, where sand dollars come from, why paddling a canoe works better when you kneel. Sometimes we didn't even talk. Just being together was enough.

The last day of camp was like a funeral. I had known Joan for only seven days, yet we'd shared a lifetime. But now she was heading back to Florida, and I was going home to Alabama. I carried her suitcase to the bus, waved good-by, and watched the trail of dust disappear down the road. Joan and I never crossed paths again.

When the week ended, a puzzle that fit perfectly was torn apart. I had to pick up the pieces and start all over again. Walking the beach and watching the ocean, I felt the waves inside myself— restless, changing, tumbling all over each other. When I desperately wanted things to stay the same, the ebb and flow of change brought emptiness and the pain of separation.

I don't know why good friends and good times come and go; why God made tides that ebb and flow, waves that never crash in exactly the same spot, sand that shifts. I don't understand why seasons come and go; why lovely green trees shed their leaves to show ugly gray branches; why the crimson red tulip has to die before it can bloom again; why the warm south winds swing around and blow cold air from the north.

What do I do with the season past? Discard it on a heap with all the other disposable, easy-come-easy-go commodities of our society and live as though life has no past or future? Should I never again venture into someone's life? I won't miss what I've never known. I'll never hurt if I never love.

Through the kaleidoscope of change I look for meaning and find that God has a purpose for every season of my life. And if God has a purpose, I am free to love even though camp ends in seven days; or graduation is only nine months away; or my neighbor may move in a year. I can reach out and embrace a new friendship without fear that it may soon end. Through it God wants me to learn, love, receive, give. I can let my roots sink deeply into the soil even though the deeper they go, the harder it will be to pull them up someday.

When things change and God turns over the well-worked soil of my experience, I know a new growing period is about to begin. That's how God works in his world, a world that never stays the same.

MARTHA'S HOUSE

M artha's house is no longer warm. It used to be a haven for me. On cold winter days, her kitchen meant a cup of hot Swiss Mocha Coffee and a blueberry muffin fresh from the oven. We would sit by the window, sip our coffee, and watch yellow finches play tag in the fir tree.

Martha's house meant people. The gold embossed guest book, always open on the table at the top of the stairs, was filled with names and addresses of people from all over the world. When I pulled into her double driveway, someone almost always had arrived ahead of me.

Today I have the driveway to myself. I pull in beside a pile of discarded plywood, a rusted bucket, and half a garden hose. The kitchen window is covered by a piece of plywood, and the fir tree is a blackened stub.

I listen for the sounds of Martha's house—the mellow ticking of the grandfather's clock that marked the hours with a chime, the chug of the electric train that weaved through the basement and entertained my ten-year-old. Voices of celebration—an engagement dinner for her son. Voices of study—forty college students jammed into the living room for discipleship classes. Sounds of a patio picnic. Sounds of a missionary home from Spain. Happy sounds. Home sounds. I listen, but all I hear today is the 9:20 commuter as it pulls into the station three blocks away. Martha's house stands cold and silent, like a stone monument against the gray sky.

The fire did its work while everyone was away. All it left was the shell—a house without a home.

"Why Martha's house?" I shake my head in disbelief as I survey the scene. "Why? When her house belonged to everyone. Why? When she gave it so generously?" As I stand and grieve over a blackened building, ashes of happy memories, I remember the words of missionary Jim Elliott, who died on the beaches of Ecuador: "He is no fool who gives what he cannot keep to gain what he cannot lose." I know Martha has kept what she will never lose. Hospitality is not contained within four walls. The spirit of Martha's house will live on, even though the shell has been destroyed.

SARA

I could not help but notice the tall, gracious, grandmotherly type woman checking groceries. Usually I read magazine covers as I stand and wait my turn, but that day I watched Sara. She seemed to be genuinely enjoying the people she served, and everyone who left her counter was smiling. As I moved closer, I heard her Southern accent and was immediately taken in, my Southern roots stirred.

I read her name tag, then called her by name. She responded warmly and asked about my day. As the frozen orange juice and Raisin Bran moved down the conveyor belt, I learned that she was from South Carolina, that she attended the University of Georgia, and that she was leaving in two weeks to visit her daughter in New York.

The conversation ended too soon.

"Have a good day, Ruth," she said, pronouncing the benediction on me as I stuffed the receipt into my purse and headed toward the door.

Apparently she read my name on my check. I was impressed that she bothered to notice.

After that day, I always looked for Sara when I was in that store. I waited for her line even if others were open. We talked about the Christmas crafts she was making, the spring flowers she was planting, or her vacation to South Carolina. Yet we still managed to get my groceries checked out and bagged without holding up the line.

One day, almost a year after we met, she told me that she and her husband attended our church and that she had known all along who I was.

Today I stare at the newspaper headlines in shock. The face of my friend Sara smiles at me from the upper right-hand corner of the page. The headline says: "Dead of gunshot wounds." I read the story four times, as though to convince myself, yet still I am not convinced. My friend Sara, murdered? My brain needs more time to absorb the reality.

I struggle with my hurt. Would I have been better off never to have learned her name or that she loved daffodils and crocheted snowflakes at Christmas? I would not be suffering as much today if she had remained "Check-out clerk. Aisle 4. Person unknown."

But in my grief for Sara I've come to understand anew that to care about people is a heavy cross to bear. It is the cross Christ chose, and for me, his follower, it is a cross that brings pain, yes, but also richness and reward. Today I have the memory of a beautiful woman who checked out groceries, enjoyed life, and loved the Lord genuinely.

TO A FRIEND IN PAIN

Today you cannot pray for
Yourself.
So I will pray for you.
Your load is too great;
It suffocates your spirit
So that you have not
Even the breath to offer your
Burden to God.
So I will lift it up for you.

Today you cannot see God.
He's lost in the blackness,
Taken a midnight flight.
So I will come to you instead.
You cannot hear his voice,
But you can hear mine.
You cannot feel his touch,
But you can feel mine.
You have no hope;
Despair has conquered
For a while.
Your days stretch before you
Like the movement of a sad
Procession
On its way to an unknown grave.
You move without expectancy
On this silent march.
You see no end to the road.
No end.
No road.
No eyes to notice.

So I will notice for you.
I will see the signs of progress you
Cannot see,
Anticipate the sun
Before it comes up,
Praise tomorrow
Before I set my alarm tonight.
Because tomorrow you will need
Signs of progress,
Anticipation,
Praise.
Because tomorrow
You will feel
Signs of regression,
Fear,
Laments.
Let me be your song,
Your sunrise,
The blank check
For your depleted resources.
"Peace I leave you . . .
Not as the world giveth . . ."
I had neither the peace
Nor the power to find it.
"Here. Let Me help you.
I can do for you
What you cannot do for yourself."
So he sent rain to my dried-up
Reservoir,
Restored my soul
So that today
I can be strong for you.

ALIEN TURF

I know of a man who walked the city streets in a pair of ratty gym shoes and a soot-gray flannel shirt. His eyes were gray too—steel gray, like the massive iron girders that hold skyscrapers aloft and pin tenement buildings to the sky. Those steel eyes could make angry men back off and make lonely children feel welcome.

As the man walked the streets in his ratty gym shoes and gray flannel shirt, he watched and listened. He saw beyond the boarded-up windows of empty store fronts. He followed the noises up narrow stairs and into desolate rooms. There he found people. People angry over absentee landlords who sat in comfortable suburbs while rats chewed on tenants; people bitter about a system that handed out menial jobs, then took all the money they earned. People too tired to fight, too desperate to hope, too crushed to care.

As he walked among people of the cold and concrete, he found their escapes. He went with them into the places where tall glasses and pretty faces helped them forget—at least for a while. He knew how they felt when they stumbled into the emptiness of night. He was there in his ratty gym shoes and gray flannel shirt to steady them.

"You get too close and you'll get yourself killed," someone told him. He knew about their switchblades and Saturday night specials. He knew the hookers and pushers. But he invaded their turf anyway. He climbed over nine-foot fences to get to them. He ignored "Keep Out" signs.

His ratty gym shoes pounded the pavement with theirs as they maneuvered a basketball down back streets and alleys. He followed them to police stations, courts, and detention homes. "You give and they'll suck the blood right out of you," someone said. But he used his own money to pay their bail.

Others had come to the city before. They came in 280Z's,

parked in the city parking garage, and caught the bus to the southside. They wore Adidas shoes and Christian Dior shirts. They brought new basketballs and hockey sticks donated by HUD or the YMCA. They came with handbook ideas on how to heal the insides of a city. When they'd made their visits, played their games, and distributed their literature, they brushed the city from their shoes and headed for the suburbs in their sports cars. And no one in the city had heard a word they said.

But when the man with the steel-gray eyes spoke, the people heard. When he knocked on doors, people let him in. And when someone ran a bullet through his head while he slept in his three-by-five tenement room, a rich suburban father grieved.

The people of the street asked, "If he had known we'd kill him, would he have come?" Some said yes. They'd heard him talk about another Man who had gone willingly to work among people he knew would kill him.

The Word became flesh and made his dwelling among us (John 1:14).

THE MYSTERY OF

◆ STRANGERS ◆

THE REMARKABLE MR. PER

S omewhere in Wisconsin lives a man named Mr. Per. The license plates on his Winnebago told us where he was from, and he told us a few other facts: he was married, he liked to fish, and he had a Persian cat named Puff. Everything else we learned about him we found out by watching.

We first spotted Mr. Per as we backed our van into campsite seven along the south shore of Bear Lake in northern Wisconsin. As we drove in, his red flannel shirt disappeared through the white birch and pine that separated our parking spot from his. "Somebody's raked our spot," Jori said, struggling with a tent pole. Sure enough, we spotted fresh rake marks in the dirt. Later we saw a rake leaning against the Winnebago.

When we returned from our after-dinner walk, we found a pile of logs stacked neatly beside our fireplace and two coloring books with crayons on the picnic table.

"Somebody likes kids," Mr. Per said quietly the next morning when I mentioned the coloring books. I knew they were from him, but I didn't press for a confession.

The next night our lantern was lit when we made our way up the path from the lake. He had hung it in perfect position to light the rocky way we had to walk. A bouquet of wildflowers in a paper cup sat on our table. As we walked into camp, we heard Mr. Per whistling through the woods, heading toward his site.

"What a nice man," Nicky commented, burying his nose in the sweet smell of cornflower and goldenrod.

The next day, we saw Mr. Per pushing through the pines toward the park bathrooms, rubber gloves, bucket, mop, and ammonia bottle in hand.

Mr. Per's graciousness knew no end. Nine-year-olds can be a hazard in a fisherman's boat, but Mr. Per invited Nicky to go fishing with him anyway. I awoke to the sound of oars on water just outside the tent. I watched as old man and youth glided across the sheet of morning sun, then anchored in the middle of the motionless lake. Nothing stirred except my heart. Who was Mr. Per, I wondered. A banker? Lawyer? Garbage collector? College professor? Auto mechanic? I didn't know, but it didn't matter. I had never met anyone who said so much about himself in so few words.

Later, Mr. Per showed Nicky how to clean the trout and cook them in a pan over the fire. Nicky proudly served us fresh fish for dinner.

On Friday we waved good-by as Mr. Per and his wife left for their next campsite. State parks were a hobby with them. I wondered who their next neighbors would be.

We did not soon forget Mr. Per. For the next few days his name came up often in conversations. By the shores of Bear Lake, our lives had been touched by a simple man who knew something profound about service. Mr. Per demonstrated for us what Jesus taught about the true spirit of giving: "But when you give . . . do not let your left hand know what your right hand is doing, so that your giving may be in secret. Then your Father, who sees what is done in secret, will reward you" (Matthew 6:3–4).

Mr. Per's kind of giving stood out to me because I live in a world of performances acted for an audience. It's easy for me to take on the same kind of role. Life too easily becomes a stage where I play out my deeds of mercy to receive personal rewards— approval, admiration, visibility. How often do I write articles, give speeches, perform the duties of parenthood, and then wonder if anyone notices how well I'm doing? Is it true mercy if I visit the grieving mother down the block and casually tell about it the next time I'm with a friend? If I take a potted plant to a woman trapped in her own apartment, afraid of the outside world, and then make her the subject of my next article, have I truly served at all, or has the result become more important than the service? Am I serving, not for what it does for the other person, but for what it does for me?

When Jesus defined giving, he singled out for criticism the religious types obsessed with public displays of service and showed them a higher standard. When he healed the deaf and dumb man, he commanded onlookers to keep quiet about what they'd seen. He often repeated the request as he moved across the countryside bringing health and wholeness. He, too, lived in a day of performers. The crowds wanted pageantry and kingdoms. He patiently reminded them that he had come for more than publicity and fanfare.

Vernon Walters, former ambassador to the United Nations, once said, "There is no end to the amount of good that can be done when one is not concerned with who gets the credit."

Mr. Per gave, I believe, not for the satisfaction of being known, but for the satisfaction of giving. I wonder, would I be so quick to serve if no one ever knew? Would I rake a campsite, stack firewood, light a lantern—then go whistling through the dark before anyone ever had a chance to say "Thanks, we knew all along it was you."

THE FOOD PANTRY THAT TALKED

I stand in the checkout line at the grocery store. Bored, as usual. I rearrange the items, making sure that the bread is on top of the orange juice and that all the cans have the labels right side up. Then I flip through a *Country Living* magazine.

A screeching noise ahead of me ends my boredom. Up and down the checkout lines, heads turn. Apparently the woman at the head of the line is unaware that her voice carries across several checkout counters.

I spot the targets of her hostility—two young teenage girls, apparently her daughers, with ghetto blasters held up to their ears. They stare blankly, straight ahead, transported by their music to some other place.

"Put those horrible things down so I can talk to you," the woman orders. The ghetto blasters do not move, but the mother continues her monologue.

"I tell you, this is the last time you ever come to the store with me. Put those things down." The radios move slightly. "You two are never satisfied, always wanting more. I'm sick and tired of your selfish attitude. Sick and tired of you. Do you hear?"

One daughter, with stooped shoulders, straight hair, and acne, nods slightly. The other glares at her mother, then looks around to see if anyone is watching. Her face flushes beet red when she realizes we are. She turns her back to her mother and faces the candy rack.

The radios go back up to their ears, but the mother continues as she unloads the cans from her cart.

"You girls need to go live in Bangladesh. Then you'd learn to appreciate what I do for you. Patty, turn that radio down and don't tell me to shush."

I want to take the girls and hide them under my coat where bitter words cannot wound. I want to tell them they're okay. The one with acne looks ready to crawl under the counter. The other still has her back toward her mother.

The woman lines her cans, exactly a dozen of each item, neatly on the conveyor belt. I wish she took such care with her daughters. Tomatoes, green beans, sweet potatoes, corn, peas, peaches, pears, spaghetti, beef stew. All arranged according to label.

She turns to the clerk, and her voice turns low and sweet. "All this food is for our missionaries. I'm in charge of the food pantry at our church. Our people give so generously. We have a real ministry."

Emotion tightens my throat. Is it anger? Pity? Righteous indignation? Embarrassment for missionary pantries around the world?

As I watch her go out the door with her precious cargo, two pained teenagers in tow, I remember God's sentiments as he pronounced judgment on a hypocritical Israel. "For I desire mercy, not sacrifice, and acknowledgment of God rather than burnt offerings" (Hosea 6:6).

I line up my groceries on the black conveyor belt and silently pray that causes will never become more important to me than people—especially the people I love most.

GARAGE ATTENDANTS
DON'T COME UP HERE

T he sixth level of the O'Hare International Airport parking garage feels more like the Sahara desert today. The sun presses down on me as I push my luggage cart rapidly along, eager for the relief of my Datsun's air conditioning. After a long day, home is uppermost in my mind. I finally reach the car, deposit my luggage in the back, and buckle myself into the driver's seat for the trip home. I turn the key, expecting a stream of cool air to relieve me within minutes from these oven-like conditions. But nothing happens. I turn the key again. Still no response. No matter how I turn the key, pump the clutch, or shift the gears, the car remains still. My Datsun has died.

Not only does it feel like the Sahara, it might as well be the Sahara. I look around for signs of life, but the only things moving are jets that streak toward the sun every sixty seconds or so. Few people park on the outer aisles of level six in the middle of the week. I look around for a button to push to summon help, but all I see are solid concrete pillars. I don't know where else to search for help.

Just then I spot a man walking the outer aisle, looking as though he has nowhere in particular to go. I wonder why he's roaming a 90-degree cement desert at mid-afternoon. He comes toward me, and I notice his red and white airport security badge. Ten years of parking in this garage and I've never seen an airport security guard.

"I don't know this territory," he says when I ask him where I might find a mechanic. "I never come up here."

I begin to feel the drama unfolding. *If you never come up here, why are you here?* I wonder, but I don't ask because I think I know the answer.

Though young, he seems to know cars. He goes deliberately to the life centers under the hood. Battery. Cables. Fluid. Belts. Plugs. "In this car the ignition is underneath," he says as he slides under the car, white shirt and all. "I believe it's your battery." His diagnosis is complete, but the only movement is still in the skies. Sweat drips from us both. "I have no idea where you'll find cables." He slams the hood in a kind of benediction. He's done all he can do. He will go on collecting luggage carts, and I will be left alone in my cement desert.

We stand for a moment in silent contemplation. Out of the corner of my eye I see a yellow flash moving slowly toward the outer aisle. Ten years of parking in this garage and I've never once seen flashing yellow. "Perfect timing," says the youth with the red badge. He waves to the brown truck with the flashing yellow light. I read "Free battery charging" on the tailgate as the vehicle of mercy pulls to a stop.

"Yes. Perfect timing," I say to him. To myself I say, *I am loved.*

"What are you doing up here?" the man behind the wheel asks the security guard.

"I don't know. Just happened to be up here collecting carts. I am a bit far from my station. Guess I needed some sun."

I know what you're doing up here, I say to myself as my engine comes to life and I wave my thanks.

Today I feel God's love. Tomorrow's dilemmas may not be so easily solved. There may be no security guard to come to my rescue. On days I do not feel God's presence, I will remember today. And if tomorrow I cannot thank God for the present, I will look back to a 90-degree day in an airport garage and thank him for the past.

THE WANDERER

He wanders up and down the narrow road,
Walking the shoulder,
Always hugging the shoulder,
His long, black hair trailing in the
Wind.
Cars whiz by; we wonder,
Whose son?
Where's he going?
Where's he been?
Maybe
He doesn't even know
For sure.
But he does.
He walks in the dust
With determined step,
Swinging his arms as he goes,
In tune with something
Or someone,
Pausing here and there
To talk to the clouds,
To swing on the goalposts
That mark the end of the field,
To pick a branch from a scrubby
Roadside shrub.
Twice he crosses the same
Parking lot
To cool himself at the
Tastee-Freeze.
Surrounded by ice-cream floats
And frosty root beers,
He only breathes the air

And goes out the door again,
His mission unknown
Except to him.
But I try to guess.
Brilliant scientist
Whose mind overdosed on facts?
A mother's son
Who didn't quite fit?
Society's reject
Tossed aside to his own illusions?
He looks both ways,
Wipes the sweat from his brow
With a big, red handkerchief,
Ties it around his wrist,
And takes to the road again.
I watch his solitary stride,
Facing the traffic head on.
He disappears from sight,
But folks say he will come again.
And I wonder
Who he is.
If he knocks on the door of an inn,
Would anyone let him in?
Did anyone let Him *in?*
Did anyone understand who He
Was?
Or did they wonder too?

THE LILY AND THE DARK

I manage to read the apartment numbers even though the hall is dark. The door I am looking for is 307. I take a deep breath, shift the Easter lily to my left hand, and knock. I don't know what to expect on the other side, and I'm not sure I'm prepared for whatever it is. A request in the mail has brought me here on this day before Easter. A new Christian who lives far away is concerned for her aunt who fears the outside world. She has not left her apartment alone for five years.

The door opens, allowing a sliver of light to come through. Above the chain lock I see a face. I feel I am looking into a cage. I speak her name softly, then her niece's name and my own, reminding her that I called the previous night to say I would be coming. She shows no sign of remembering, but when I repeat her name she reaches up and unbolts the door.

I walk into a tomb, of sorts. A cold room full of shadows. She doesn't turn on a lamp. I can make out a crucifix hanging between two baskets of plastic flowers on the opposite wall. The TV gives off light but no sound. I put the Easter lily on the coffee table next to a framed picture of Christ on the cross. Rosary beads drape the frame. My lily looks out of place, but I don't know where else to set it.

We skip the polite formalities. She suspects I am here for a reason. "I don't have nothing to do with religion. It made me sick. Every time I prayed, I cried; I felt so guilty. Ended up in a psych hospital. Doctors told me not to pray anymore." She seems to fade into the dusk and then suddenly reappear.

"You're not one of those born-again ones, are you? I have no time for them. My sister stole my husband. Now she comes wanting to talk to me about being born again. No sir. You can keep that born-again stuff."

She doesn't wait for a response. While she talks I sit silently in a green overstuffed chair thinking I might as well *be* the chair. Every now and then I speak, but she makes it clear that she wants to do the talking.

"It's been eight years since I've seen two of my children. One comes every month, brings my groceries, sets them on the table, then leaves." I notice a shelf of pictures in gold frames—apparently the closest she comes to having relationships.

After listening for an hour and a half, I feel as if I have walked through a Greek tragedy. The dark is settling in, but we are still without a light in the room. In the dusk I see the lily. It still looks out of place.

When I rise to go I ask if I might pray. She doesn't object but starts to cry in the middle of my prayer.

"Please come back. Please be my friend." She holds tightly to my hand. I promise to come again. On the way to the door I pass the crucifix. The thought occurs to me that Easter has not yet come to this place. Christ is still on the cross. She lives without hope.

The door closes behind me. She returns to the prison of her mind, and I walk out into the soft April evening. The sky is spread with stars. I think of the one who came to "set the captives free."

No, the lily is not out of place in apartment 307. It's exactly where it belongs. Oh that I might walk more often among the captives. For in so doing, we both learn about freedom.

GARFIELD

I could tell he was nervous when he entered the plane. A purple half-shirt covered part of his body, long blond hair screened most of his face, and sunglasses covered his eyes. They hid his identity, but not his anxiety.

"I'm on my way to the Garfield School in Denver," he announced loudly to the flight attendant as he entered the aircraft just ahead of me.

"You ever heard of the Garfield School?" the bemused stewardess asked me.

"Can't say that I have. The only Garfield I know is a cat." We both laughed.

Those of us who wore navy suits and carried burgundy briefcases shared a certain camaraderie. We had little in common with anyone who wore purple half-shirts and a single black leather glove with the fingertips cut off.

While the rest of the passengers settled in, Garfield walked the aisles.

"Could you find a window seat for me?" he asked the flight attendant. "I think I might get sick if I can't see out."

By now, Garfield had captured the full attention of the passengers. We looked on, amused.

"Garfield wants to know where the smoking section is." A second flight attendant entered the drama. Apparently word had spread about Garfield.

His next trip up the aisle was to ask for help with his straw bag, which was too big to fit under the seat. He had planned on holding it, he said. Couldn't understand how holding it would hurt anyone. The straw bag ended up under the seat.

The flight attendant wiped her forehead as she returned to the bulkhead.

"The guy's never flown," she chuckled to those of us within earshot. "This could be interesting."

For me, the drama with Garfield started inside the terminal. The woman standing beside him looked old—much older than I guessed her age to be—and her gray hair poked out in all directions. During most of the thirty-minute wait she stood and stared at the DC-10 parked at the gate.

"What a bird," she muttered, as much to herself as to anyone. The purple shirt beside her never replied. Neither mother nor son seemed to notice anything but the plane. They spoke no other words to each other. When it came time to board, Garfield was one of the first in line.

The woman moved with him to the door. While some of us hugged and whispered tender good-bys to loved ones, Garfield's mother raised her hand to her son's shoulder. Then, with more of a push than a hug, she pronounced her parental benediction. "Kid, you're on your own now."

She turned toward us.

"Finally, he's gone!" Her words came out in a long relieved sigh, as if it had been stored inside her for her son's lifetime. Garfield never looked back. He marched forward toward the big bird and Denver. He never even said good-by.

Hours later, as my children wrap their arms of "welcome home" around me, I remember Garfield. When did the mother-son silence start, I wonder. Long before the airport scene, no doubt. Probably over something inconsequential, like dust under his bed or purple half-shirts. Parent-child blowouts don't usually start with a loud bang. They begin as a small leak in communication.

"I'm so glad to be your mom," I say to the children as I tuck them into bed.

Someday I'll tell them the story of Garfield. But tonight we talk about the "king and queen" rock formations that I saw while flying over Monument Valley, about the goal Nicky scored in soccer, and about the *B* Jori got on her English test.

As I turn out their lights I think about a purple half-shirt, a black leather glove with fingers sticking out, and a mom who said, "Finally, he's gone." No wonder they had nothing more to say to each other.

LESSONS FROM A COFFEE COUNTER

U nion Station looks as if it has never slept. The California Zephyr from San Francisco backs onto track 1, and the Burlington Commuter Line empties work-bound passengers on platform 7. The passageways are jammed. We arrive at the gates just in time to hear the announcement that the Broadway Limited from New York is an hour late. The kids head for the video arcade, quarters jingling in their pockets, and Mark and I grab the next two available stools at the coffee counter. All of Union Station, it seems, flows through this point. It's a people watcher's paradise.

I order my coffee black and my doughnut without sugar. The waitress sets my coffee in front of me and reaches under the counter for a spoon. "Thank you, Thelma," I say as she heads the other way. At the sound of her name she spins around and looks me in the eye for the first time. "Not many people bother to read my nametag," she says. Her black face breaks into a broad grin as she goes to her next customer. In no time she is back, propping her elbows on the counter's edge as though she intends to stay.

"So you're a Bear's fan," Mark says, nodding at her navy stocking cap that proclaims, in bright orange, "This is Chicago Bear Country." She talks about her ten-year-old grandson who lives with her and watches every game. "I can't help but be a fan," she adds. "We watch together. Poor child has no one else."

Thelma refills our cups even though mine is still three-quarters full. She glances down the counter. "Yes, ma'am, I've been coming to this here corner for fifteen years now, every morning of the year at 5:30. Very few people like to talk. They too busy. But I could write a book about 'em. Maybe I will someday. Sure would be better than pouring coffee."

She shuffles down the row to collect her tips and wipe the counter. When she returns she tells us about her customer who pours jelly beans on his buttermilk pancakes every morning. And about the fur-wrapped woman who sat down one morning, looked at the menu, then asked, "Isn't this the Mademoiselle Dress Shop?" Thelma slaps the counter and laughs when she tells it. I notice a front tooth is missing.

The hour goes quickly. The children have returned, their quarters depleted. Thelma has talked and refilled our cups the entire time. We stand to leave when we hear the Broadway Limited announced on track 2. "You come back now," she says as she picks up Mark's generous tip. "And have a safe trip." I don't bother to tell her we aren't going anywhere.

As we look through the crowd for Grandma and Grandpa I think of all the Thelmas in the world. Each with stories to tell if only someone would ask. I think too of the man who sat one day near a well, the local watering hole, and took time to show an interest in the woman he met there (see John 4). I determine I will ask people questions more often.

EPILOGUE

I watch for you among the hurried travelers
Who push their luggage carts down F concourse
Toward the baggage claim.
You are here,
Among the crowd,
Perhaps standing by a coffee counter
Drinking hot tea with just a bit of cream.
Or stopping to buy stamps
To send messages to the ones you love.
This is your airport.
You travel it often.
You are here among us.
But you are not one of us.

I look for you among the clouds
That form just outside the window of the DC-10,
So close I think I can scoop them up
And take them home for our nature collection.
You have ridden these clouds
Circuited these winds
Scouted this vast expanse on which we hang.
This is your route.
You travel these airways.
You hide yourself among the clouds.
But you are higher than the clouds.

I look for you among the hills
Covered by Douglas fir
And redwood pine.
You have picked this rhododendron bloom
Traced this beetle in the sand
Felt this wind blow in your face.

This is your creation.
You walk these paths.
Yet, really, you walked only one path—
To a cross.

Lord,
The greatest paradox of all,
You are God
With us
But above us.
In us
But not of us.
A God I know
Yet above all knowing
Wrapped in mystery.
Worthy of praise.

A NOTE TO THE READER

This book was selected by the same editors who prepare *Guideposts*, a monthly magazine filled with true stories of people's adventures in faith.

If you have found inspiration in this book, we think you'll find monthly help and inspiration in the exciting stories that appear in our magazine.

Guideposts is not sold on the newsstand. It's available by subscription only. And subscribing is easy. All you have to do is write Guideposts Associates, Inc., 39 Seminary Hill Road, Carmel, New York 10512. A year's subscription costs only $8.95 in the United States, $10.95 in Canada and overseas.

When you subscribe, each month you can count on receiving exciting new evidence of God's presence and His abiding love for His people.